Helen Hayward Jones is a freelance writer with an extensive background in both broadcasting and college training. She has trained manual writers at IBM and has taught writing at a major insurance company, a hospital, and at Meredith College in North Carolina.

PRENTICE-HALL INTERNATIONAL, INC., London
PRENTICE-HALL OF AUSTRALIA PTY. LIMITED, Sydney
PRENTICE-HALL CANADA INC., Toronto
PRENTICE-HALL OF INDIA PRIVATE LIMITED, New Delhi
PRENTICE-HALL OF JAPAN, INC., Tokyo
PRENTICE-HALL OF SOUTHEAST ASIA PTE. LTD., Singapore
WHITEHALL BOOKS LIMITED, Wellington, New Zealand
EDITORA PRENTICE-HALL DO BRASIL LTDA., Rio de Janeiro

PROGRAMMING
BETTER
WRITING

HOW TO DEVELOP
EFFECTIVE WRITING SKILLS
FOR A COMPUTERIZED AGE

HELEN HAYWARD JONES

A SPECTRUM BOOK

Prentice-Hall, Inc., Englewood Cliffs, New Jersey 07632

Library of Congress Cataloging in Publication Data

Jones, Helen Hayward.
    Programming better writing.

    "A Spectrum Book."
    Bibliography: p.
    Includes index.
    1. English language—Rhetoric.   I. Title.
PE1408.J82   1983   808′.042   83-4417
ISBN 0-13-729897-8
ISBN 0-13-729889-7 (pbk.)

10 9 8 7 6 5 4 3 2 1

ISBN 0-13-729897-8

ISBN 0-13-729889-7 {PBK.}

Editorial/production supervision by Chris McMorrow
Cover design © 1983 by Jeannette Jacobs
Manufacturing buyer: Christine Johnston

This book is available at a special discount when ordered in
bulk quantities. Contact Prentice-Hall, Inc., General
Publishing Division, Special Sales, Englewood Cliffs, N.J. 07632.

TO MY FAMILY

CONTENTS

PREFACE

This book on writing is for people who like clear guidelines that lead to *appreciable* results.

We think that includes a good many people—students whose skills are limited by an inadequate educational background, adults for whom writing is a professional requirement, instructors who'd like to see more students able to communicate on paper. *Programming Better Writing* puts handles on writing skills that are easily grasped, that can be effectively taught or learned alone.

What it does. *Programming Better Writing* presents long-proved principles in a unique and contemporary form. Its simple system effects clear organization, not only of writing, but—eventually—of the reader's thinking processes. Founded on bedrock principles, its steps are set within a fresh and inviting context that includes the following:

1. A logical and consistent analogy between its writing process and that followed by the computer programmer.
2. Three flexible essay patterns that afford most students a measure of immediate success. (One of them serves to organize this preface.)
3. Unusual real-life illustrations that present lively, personable individuals in a variety of writing situations.

In its two final chapters, *Programming Better Writing* discusses some basic writing problems specific to management writing, including various means by which psychological strategies are effected.

Why it works. The plan presented by *Programming Better Writing* works for the soundest of reasons: It teaches patterns based on human thought processes. Scientific studies tell us that perception is a matter of forming patterns, that we assimilate best what is presented in top-down order from general to specific. We all know, too, that we delight in a gimmick—if it helps us to remember.

Let's look at explanations of these three points.

1. Gestalt psychology (no longer a theory) insists that we form patterns in everything we do. We learn to drive—or type, or dance, or play golf—with conscious effort; soon those continuing responses slide into our subconscious and we repeat them without thinking. Our actions become so consistent that we betray ourselves. Not just the criminal with his M.O., nor the victim with his punctual drive to the bank with the day's receipts—rather, each one of us fixates much or most of what we do. If we write often enough, we establish writing patterns. Why, then, should they not be patterns that achieve optimal communication?

Nay-sayers will protest the possible loss of the individual's "voice." Any loss occasioned is no greater than that in a comparable art, say, music. Does the gifted coloratura suffer loss by learning the mathematics of harmony? Or the painter, by observing the angles of perspective? Communication in any art, we think, rises strongest from basic patterns that are *shared*. Beginning writers are more likely to be silent, in Wordsworth's words, from having "felt the weight of too much liberty."

2. Both for humans who program computer intelligence and for humans who write for another human intelligence, communication is best achieved in top-down order, as major problems are solved, as responsibility is delegated. This is the order imposed by the process of perception—from the whole gestalt to its parts, from general to specific (just as most textbooks are designed). To use top-down order consistently in writing requires a disciplined mind, not ordinarily developed early in life. *Programming Better Writing* can teach top-down order because of a simple guide, a limited set of steps by which even beginning writers can produce desirable clarity.

3. In addition, *Programming Better Writing* includes a unique mnemonic device—a gimmick to help you remember its points. It presents its patterns in three's—three basic patterns, each with three divisions, three examples, and so on. Although few people realize the prevalence of triads, *three* seems to be our favorite numerical grouping. Triads are notable in the tenets of major religions, in patriotic exhortations, in folklore and nursery rhymes, and—perhaps the cause of all the rest—in nature, as in sun, moon, and stars.

Such effective resources as these have worked in college classrooms and business environments for a dozen years. In *Programming Better Writing* you'll find they will work for you.

Gramatti's words in the epigraph section are taken from "A Talk with A. Barlett Gramatti," in *The College Board Review,* Spring 1982, and are quoted by permission.

Brian W. Kernighan and P.J. Plauger's quote is taken from *The Elements of Programming Style,* 1st edition, © 1974 by McGraw-Hill Book Company and is reproduced with permission.

The excerpt from Peter Calvocaressi, *Top Secret Ultra,* © 1981 by Pantheon Books, a Division of Random House, Inc. is used by permission.

Material from David W. Ewing, *Writing for Results* (New York: John Wiley & Sons, 1974) © 1974 by John Wiley & Sons, is quoted by permission.

The excerpt from Eric Berne, *What Do You Say After You Say Hello?* © 1972 by Eric Berne, M.D., is reprinted by permission of Random House.

Material from *Encyclopedia of Computer Science* by Anthony Ralston, copyright © 1976 by Van Nostrand Reinhold Company, is reprinted by permission of the publisher.

The sections from Paul Bryan, *Programming Your Computer* (Blue Ridge Summit, PA: Tab Books, 1982) and Michael Hordeski, *Illustrated Dictionary of Microcomputer Terminology* (Blue Ridge Summit, PA.: Tab Books, 1981) are quoted by permission.

A paraphrase of Raphael Rhodes' explanation of hypnotism is taken from Raphael Rhodes, *Hypnosis: Theory, Practice, and Application* (Secaucus, N.J.: Citadel Press, 1950), and is cited by permission.

Excerpts from Thomas Whiteside, *Computer Capers* (New York: Harper & Row, 1978) (Thomas Y. Crowell) are reprinted by permission of Harper & Row, Publishers, Inc., and Sidgwick & Jackson, Ltd., London.

The excerpt from Paul Friedman, *Computer Programs in Basic,* © 1981 by Paul Friedman, published by Prentice-Hall, Inc., Englewood Cliffs, N.J. 07632 is used by permission.

Portions of Thom Hill's essay "GE Has Big Plans for Microelectronics" are quoted by permission of the *News & Observer of Raleigh.*

The excerpt from "Citadel on a Hill" is reprinted by permission from TIME, copyright 1981 Time Inc. All rights reserved.

The quotation cited in the epigraph and other material from Dennie Van Tassel, *Program Style, Design, Efficiency, Debugging, and Testing,* 2nd ed., (Englewood Cliffs, N.J.: Prentice-Hall, © 1978) are reprinted by permission.

Material from Gordon B. Davis, *Introduction to Computers* (New York: McGraw-Hill, 1977), is quoted by permission.

Excerpts from Charles L. Howe, "Coping with Computer Criminals," *Datamation,* 28, no. 1 (January 1982) is quoted by permission.

A passage from Herman M. Weisman, *Technical Correspondence: A Handbook and Reference Source for the Technical Professional,* © 1968 by Herman Weisman, is quoted by permission of John Wiley & Sons.

The "Structure Tree" from Marilyn Bohl's *A Guide for Programmers* (Englewood Cliffs, N.J.: Prentice-Hall, Inc., © 1978), is reprinted by permission.

There's no point in kidding oneself that an awful lot of kids at the ages of 18 and 22 do not come to college prepared to organize a page of prose as well as they used to.

A. Bartlett Gramatti
President of Yale University

The form and approach of this [manual of computer programming style] have been strongly influenced by *The Elements of Style* [in writing] by W. Strunk and E.B. White.

Brian W. Kernigham and P.J. Plauger,
in preface to *The Elements of Programming Style*

Top-down program design is similar to top-down [business or professional] report writing. . . . The most important step in having an efficient and correct program occurs before the program is written. It is the selection of the best algorithm for the purpose.

Dennie Van Tassel, *Program Style, Design, Efficiency, Debugging, and Testing*

1
SOLVING THE PROBLEM OF WRITING: A SHORT CUT

GOAL: To understand that what we know about programming a computer can "program" your reader to follow your written message

You are probably an active person, like most Americans. Caught up in the whirl of various demands, perhaps you've had little time for polishing the slow skills of writing.

Sometimes, however, you find yourself having to write—a term paper on which your grade depends, a blistering complaint to the City Council, a sales presentation that should earn you a raise.

At times like these, you face a problem. Moreover, it's a touchy problem, for its solution exposes your thinking to someone's critical judgment.

Perhaps the entire process dismays you: You must evoke the appropriate thought, clothe it with supportive explanation, and transfer it to paper. Even with your best efforts, you may feel some trepidation as you send it forth, a sort of unready hostage to fortune.

How can you make the process of writing less stressful?

This book provides a short cut that will help you.

It offers a pattern for the most useful kind of exposition—writing that requires a stated opinion, sufficiently justified and developed. Within this category lie not only academic papers and most books that are not fiction, but speeches, news writing, all business communication. Such exposition stitches together the fabric of the world's work.

Like all human problem solving, written communication results from a continuing process of selection. The programmed writing you'll find here enables you most often to make a good choice—or at least a choice that almost invariably gets the job done satisfactorily.

The pattern this book presents resembles the highway a friend marks for you on a road map. In following it, you ramble less than if you strike out on your own. And you can be comfortably sure of reaching your destination.

THE COVER SENTENCE:
ITS PROOF PHRASE

Would you say that you can write the main thought of your term paper, your complaint to the City Council, or your sales promotion in this form?

> So-and-so is such-and-such *for three reasons.*

Yes, of course you can. Here is an easy example.

> A job should be more than a way to pay your bills (*for three reasons*).

To find and write such a clear statement as this is the key to the *program plan.*
This crucial statement involves pinning down three components:

> *A Subject:* Whatever you wish to explain or justify
> *A Focus on That Subject:* A predication about that subject; that is, your opinion of it
> *Sufficient Support for That Opinion:* Three elements that will section your explanation

Here, the job, of course, is your subject. (In a beginning composition class a teacher might ask you to write a paragraph on your personal philosophy concerning jobs.) After some thought you are able to state an opinion about it: should be more than a way to pay your bills. Because many people think of a job only in terms of a paycheck, such a statement cannot stand on your unsupported word; you must support it with proof: for three reasons. That is, you contract with your reader to supply three different areas of proof.

Here are examples of the PROOF statement that are more complex:

1. For a communications major, the intern program offered by KXZR will provide three marketable skills.
2. The custom of business conventions clearly reflects certain basic drives of professional Americans: *their gregariousness, their urge to exchange business secrets,* and *their zeal for self-improvement.*
3. The tragedy of the ill-starred Empress Carlotta develops *in three geographical stages:* at Miramar, at Chapultepec, and at Queretaro.

You'll note in these examples that the *proof* statement may suggest the elements of the justifying phrase, as in (1), or it can specify or name them, as in (2), or it can do both, as seen in (3). Sometimes the three supports are integral to the predication, as in (4), or omitted altogether, as in (5).

4. For a communications major, the intern program offered at KXZR provides *three benefits*.
5. The custom of holding business conventions clearly reflects *certain basic drives* of professional Americans.

Important: Where the *proof phrase* is omitted, the sentence should be worded so that the phrase *could be added*. Given a satisfactory topic, it is this particular form or structure of the sentence that assures you of a viable thesis, a thought that offers room for expansion.

The Statement's Versatility

As you note also from the examples, the *proof phrase* can represent three divisions of almost anything:

	because of three factors
	through three methods
So-and-so is (or does) such-and-such	*as three types*
or	*with three characteristics*
The reader should think such-and-such	*by three examples*
	from three causes
	at three levels

Thus, such a proof phrase can suggest either of the two broad classes into which virtually all reports or essays fall:

INFORMATION OR ANALYSIS:

Ex.: A well-posed problem has three basic requirements.

JUSTIFICATION OR PERSUASION:

Ex.: Learning to write clearly teaches good thinking on three levels.

Worded as we suggest, with the proof phrase included or implied, the cover statement maps the broad divisions of your report. You have only to explain each division in turn and to provide examples.

As you'll see, our cover sentence provides a reliable short cut to *top-down* development, that is, the descent of thought from the general to the particular (often referred to as deductive development). Although this ordering of facts is acknowledged to provide optimal clarity in written communication, the average person seldom learns its skills. *Without the short cut this book provides, such a logical presentation of facts requires a disciplined mind,* usually not achieved until long after the individual has settled into "doing his own thing" in the area of writing.

Teaching practices that emphasize such self-expression ("doing one's own thing") are less popular now than they were five years ago. Today's tight job market lends emphasis to the annoyed complaints of a decade of employers: Many college graduates cannot write. If your communication skills fall short of your future needs, this *program plan* can serve as a bridge to a securer future.

The Reliability of Three Proofs

Why do we insist on *three* divisions of the *proof phrase?*

Actually, our plan works as well for two proofs, or for four. You should certainly determine the number of your paper's divisions according to the available material. For the average college student, however, we find that our requirement for three divisions acts as insurance for adequate expansion. To fill the suggested slots, the person who has trouble expanding on his basic thought is encouraged to generate more support than he would otherwise. On the other hand, the need to reduce the divisions to three also prevents him from skimming off a stringy five or six; thus, he learns the important logic of subordination. Certainly a few good points, well developed, carry more impact than a long, spindly, ill-assorted list.

Moreover, the number *three* has its own significant power. To the reader's subconscious, *three* is usually accepted as sufficiency, neither too few nor too many, but satisfyingly right. Such scientists as Sigmund Freud and Bruno Bettelheim discuss our mysterious reaction to a triad's sufficiency, noting its pervasive presence in world religions, in folklore, in patriotic exhortation, in logic. Perhaps the surprising number of triads in nature are reflected in our collective unconscious.

At any rate, let us agree that you will begin your reports or essays henceforth with a *cover statement* that contains or suggests a *proof phrase*.

The Cover Statement's Flexibility

Another benefit delivered by the *program plan* is that of its versatility. Once you have learned to word your cover sentence in terms of a subject, a focus on that subject, and a proof phrase, you can generate not only a wide variety of writing, but also writing of different lengths and complexity. Let's consider again that group of cover sentences given earlier.

> A job should be more than a way to pay your bills (for three reasons).
>
> For a communications major, the intern program offered by KXZR will provide three marketable skills.
>
> The custom of business conventions clearly reflects basic drives of professional Americans: their gregariousness, their urge to exchange business secrets, and their zeal for self-improvement.
>
> The tragedy of the ill-starred Empress Carlotta develops in three geographical areas: at Miramar, at Chapultepec, and at Queretano.

Built into each of these sentences is the promise of a discussion not only divided into three parts, but also of sufficient amplitude to justify the thought it voices.

Thus, while the justification of a job's benefits would extend to no more than a single paragraph of less than a handwritten page, the succeeding cover statements promise a much longer discussion. The one about the broadcasting internship suggests a feature story in a college newspaper of about five short paragraphs. The thesis dealing with professional conventions, originally published in *Fortune* (August, 1954), covered almost four large two-column pages. The sentence about Carlotta represents the broad organization of a full-length biography, *The Cactus Throne,* by Richard O'Connor (1971).

The organizational benefits delivered by the cover sentence of our *program plan* do not stop once the three broad divisions are designated. In a long article like that on business conventions, similar but lower-level sentences continue to section each of the three divisions into individual modules, until finally each paragraph is developed from its topic sentence. In practice, this kind of sectioning is highly convenient as well as practical. It enables you, the writer, to prepare three nicely organized compositions one at a time, which eventually you bring together with an introduction and conclusion.

Many people go about writing a paper of fifteen or twenty pages as if they were framing a house the traditional way—rough interior divisions along with the outer wall supports. By contrast, the *program plan* enables you to construct three pre-built modules—and then fit them together at your chosen site.

SCIENTIFIC SUPPORT
FOR THE PROGRAM PLAN

Our continuing stress on the cover sentence and its phrasing will possibly surprise you. In your English classes, such overviews as topic sentence and essay thesis may not have been required. In that case, it is also likely that you've had no guidelines to the internal structure of paragraphs, guidelines that our *program plan* so effectively supplies.

Suppose, then, we touch on the psychological basis for the top-down presentation of an idea or thesis.

Behind our emphasis on hierarchical development stands the issue of perception. (Perception, we remind you, includes not only what is visible, but what is discernible by all the senses and the mind. That is, a parent perceives not only an infant's screaming, but also the cause of the screaming—an open safety pin.) With very few exceptions, the writer's goal is to present his ideas so that they are wholly perceived (and then accepted) by the reader.

On any level of skill, the writer must present his thoughts in one of three possibilities—quite simply: up, down, or around.

He can develop his examples and arguments first, concluding with the point they have established.

He can state his thesis and then develop its supports in hierarchical descent, as we do here.

He can be circuitous, either by design or lack of concern, stating the thesis somewhere along the way (or letting the reader draw his own conclusions).

Current studies that uphold top-down development make three concepts very clear: (1) we perceive first the "whole" of what we experience, and then its parts; (2) in reading, we formulate an expectation of the writer's meaning, *then* we verify it from the individual marks; and (3) the human brain is itself hierarchical and organizes complexities hierarchically.

1. That we perceive an entire configuration or "whole" is well-established gestalt psychology. We experience the pleasant taste of ice cream; we do not add together its coldness, it sweetness, its texture, as was thought until this century. We recognize an equilateral triangle or a square before we estimate its angles. We learn the conjugation of a French verb or the procedure for extracting square roots by forming a gestalt or pattern of each step.

Gestalt psychology supports our *program plan* in two additional concepts: (a) We analyze what we perceive "from above down" (a much-quoted phrase), progressing from large divisions to small. (b) We fixate patterns of what we perceive. On a conscious level, we learn a certain configuration; with repetition it is gradually transferred to automatic or subconscious control and rendered semi-permanent.

(These references to gestalt psychology are necessarily generalized and brief. Most psychology textbooks or a good encyclopedia will provide detailed explanations.)

2. As in perception, a reader formulates a "whole" of his progressive expectations and then perceives the inchoate hypothesis verified or disappointed.

Formerly, readers were thought to "sound out" syllables in their mind and then process the words as they would with oral language. Instead, writes Russell A. Hunt in *College English,* "the process is almost the exact opposite ... ; the reader works much more frequently from meaning down [rather] than from graphic display up."[1] Drawing on personal experience, inferences, and attitudes, the reader forms subconscious expectations of the material to come. "These expectations ... are based on and tested against a hierarchy of cues in the text, cues that range from grammatical-syntactic ... to longer-term, pragmatic matters like organization and tone and purpose."[2]

3. The brain itself is hierarchical, says George Edgin Pugh, president of Decision-Science Applications, formerly a professor of physics at Massachusetts Institute of Technology, and a member of the Institute of Defense Analysis. In *The Biological Origin of Human Values* he asserts that the brain solves problems by attacking them hierarchically. As Gestalt principles imply, it comprehends most effectively those complexities that are presented in hierarchical order.[3]

To explain, he cites a problem incurred in the early sixties before scientists considered hierarchy an essential factor in programming artificial intelligence.

Serving with the Institute of Defense Analysis, he and other members sought to design a highly complex artificial intelligence system such that it would control the fate of a fleet of bombers. The number of variables to be included was intimidating. What decisions must the system make as to kind and degree of disasters incurred, according to the number of planes involved and the distance remaining to the target? Was a plane to seek a secondary target? Under what circumstances must a mission be aborted? At any given stage, which received primary consideration, the plane and crew, or reaching the target?

Because top brass were determined to include certain specifics at the critical design level, the designers tried repeatedly to avoid a hierarchical design. Finally, the team pronounced hierarchy essential—and it has proved to be essential ever since.

What all this suggests for us, then, is the need to make the controlling thought clear almost immediately in your paper, so that the reader can properly classify the information that follows. Few of us care to involve top-level thinking processes in sorting out a mixed bag. To require your reader to do so is to indicate a certain lack of consideration, both for him and for your message.

If, like a teacher or an office supervisor, he must pursue your intended meaning through an obstacle course of confusion, he may reject your good idea along with its expression.

It is in your interest, obviously, to consider his.

THE COMPUTER ANALOGY

In this book we are led to speak of *programming* successful writing because of the research done by Pugh and others like him. Such scientists point out the parallels between the decision-making of artificial intelligence and that of the human mind. If it is possible to program a computer to arrive at a wide range of human-like decisions, then similar processes should "program" your reader to act according to your directions; that is, to think as you direct. After all, why do you write? Certainly it is to lead your reader to follow the direction of your thought.

While the artificial intelligence of which Pugh writes is far more advanced than that of industrial computers, the latter are sufficiently similar to the human mind to bear a number of comparisons. The following comparison table is based on information from Pugh.

THE HUMAN BRAIN	THE COMPUTER'S CENTRAL PROCESSING UNIT
Localized areas for certain functions	*Localized devices* for certain functions
Reasoning powers that assess and solve problems	*Processor* that decodes the problem and calculates the solution
Memory—information from books, experience, other people	*Memory*—items of information stored not only in the CPU but on disks, tape, drums
Judgment, innate logic—reasoning abilities	*Control*—a governor that makes sure instructions are obeyed in sequence
Nerves that direct *eyes, ears*	*Input* devices that accept instructions
Nerves to *hands* that write or type	*Output* devices that print the solution on a screen or typewriter, etc.

It is hardly surprising that, in building bigger and better computers, scientists have considerably increased their understanding of the human brain. Discussing the parallels offered by artificial intelligence, Pugh writes, "To develop an understanding of some of the problems [of a human decision system], we will depend heavily on the analogy with the artificial, or computerized, systems."

He goes on to say,

> These computerized systems exhibit many of the properties usually associated with intelligent adaptive behavior. They make choices in terms of an internal value scale. When confronted with changes in the environment, they exhibit very systematic and purposeful behavior.[4]

Just as laboratory animals serve to explain human physiological reactions, so what we know of the computer's artificial intelligence will guide us to optimal methods of writing to be read.

The electronic processes by which the computer "inputs" information and decodes it, then, roughly correspond to those of your reader's mind. The differences lie in the kinds of thought processes made explicit by the two sets of instructions. All steps in the computer program appear in computer (machine) language; the sentences in your paper, obviously, appear in the symbols of an English word. Each instruction to the computer results in an arithmetical procedure; each of your sentences should result in an advance in a logical train of thought.

The computer, of course, does not judge the material it reads. If the program is cumbersome and long-winded, it can't grumble, "I don't like these sloppy directions! You didn't work hard enough to make them orderly and concise!" It can only give up and break down.

(In some cases, the workshop for doctoring a sick computer is housed close to it in the same room.)

The person who reads your paper can—and will—pass judgment!

The Algorithm

In the initial steps of writing an important paper, the careful writer follows much the same procedure as the highly skilled professional who prepares a computer program. First, both must determine the nature of the problem and its requirements. Second, both must decide on the steps by which to present their material.

Thus, the writer begins by making sure he will be following the requirements. What subjects shall be considered? How broad shall the focus be? How shall it be slanted? Are adequate resources available?

The writer who follows the *program plan* knows the reliable steps by which to direct the reader's mind. In the various divisions of the paper he will follow *top-down* order:

> cover sentence
> main-point statement
> explanation
> specific example

The programmer, too, begins by defining the problem. He ascertains what must be accomplished, the form and type of input data, the output required. That finished, the programmer must settle on the steps that he directs the computer to perform. These are a series of arithmetical operations, comparable to the logical responses your sentences elicit from your reader. The programmer's steps appear as an algebraic equation that is known as an *algorithm*.

Algorithm (al go rithm) is an ancient Arabic term, now very much an "in" word with the computer-minded public. The *Dictionary of Microcomputers* (1981) defines the term as follows:

> Algorithm: A series of instructions or procedural steps designed to result in the solution of a specific problem.

Other dictionaries tell us that the steps must be limited to a certain number, and that they must be recursive. (*Recursive* means that any of the steps may be repeated as the writer desires.) In addition, an algorithm is designed to handle not just a single isolated problem, but a range of data.

Because of the similarities between the human mind and the digital computer, these qualifications for the programmer's algorithm apply equally well to our *program plan*. Our set of steps is procedural; it solves the problem of conveying information understandably to a reader. Most often the steps are four in number, although you will see later that they may be as few as three or as many as five, depending on the depth of the writer's discussion. Any or all of the steps are recursive, as is evident in the next chaper when we expand the algorithm into a short paper.

Moreover, the algorithm the programmer devises usually represents the most economical use of the computer's time. As you remember, our *top-down* steps represent the optimal clarity in presenting information to a reader, therefore the most economical use of his time.

Thus, we find it wholly reasonable to refer to our steps as an *algorithm*. This romantic-sounding word will remind you of the potential benefits available to transform your writing problems.

Before we develop a paragraph from our algorithm, suppose we supply a simple analogy that indicates how natural and logical you will find it. In this real-life scene, you will follow the familiar processing of raw material (that possessing the largest *number* of possible uses) to the finished, *specific* item. This process parallels the steps of our algorithm as they descend from the most general thought (that implying the largest number of details) to the most specific.

HENRY'S GEMSTONES AS PROCESS

Let us introduce Henry, a rockhound—a roaming rockhound.

Weekdays, rangy, pleasant-faced Henry sits at a desk in an accountant's office like any young executive. Weekends and vacations, however, find Henry anywhere from Maine to Carolina to Wyoming—wherever gemstones may be found.

In hard-hat and steel-toed shoes, Henry pokes through rock quarries, stream beds, fresh-cut roadways. Worming his long body through crevices, he explores moist, dark tunnels of old mines, alert to a special ring of steel on stone, the promise of a hollow-sounding rock.

Just now, you see him in his hometown museum, setting up a display of the best of his hard-won collection—native American rubies, sapphires, and emeralds.

He has brought the tissue-wrapped stones for the exhibit in a heavy black crystal matrix, a hollowed-out rectangular chunk of polished quartz, smoky as roiling thunderclouds. Its suitability as a backdrop for the bright gemstones pleases Henry, for many of his treasures budded in a crevice of glassy quartz.

Thus, because it represents the natural bed that enclosed the gems, this caddy is particularly appropriate to begin his display. He will lay out the stones in the logical progression: from the raw chunk that he prized from its first crystal nest, through the ongoing processes that finally result in the ring-sized jewel.

Noting with approval that the fan-shaped display case has been neatly floored with dull gold foil, Henry centers the emptied quartz matrix at the far end. With careful hands he removes the glowing rubies from their protective tissue, admiring their good, deep crimson—almost the pigeon-blood of the most prized Burmese stones.

Down and to the right of the smoky quartz he places the "rough," the stone as nature formed it in its ancient bed—a fist-sized chunk of dichroic ruby that refracts two rays of light. From this side, the faces glow in typical deep carmine;

when he steps two paces to his left, the stone becomes a surprising reddish orange.

Now for the preforms, he thinks—the button-sized selects that have been cut from the rough in varous shapes, then subjected to eight weeks of continuous slow tumbling. By the harsh friction against gravel, the stones have been punished smooth and gradually polished, each a preview of the eventual jewel. Henry lays out six of the best ovals and ellipses, spacing them down from the dichroic chunk and to its right. They lie there against the dull gold foil like shining gouts of blood.

At the bottom of the display case, nearest Henry and future viewers, he begins the fourth and final step—a dozen rubies professionally cut, fulfilling the promise hinted at in that first rough chunk. Three are as large as hazelnuts, domed *en cabochon* to show their six-rayed stars; the others—like small braziers of glowing fire—have been faceted.

At this stage, we will interrupt Henry to make several points in our analogy.

1. (a) The smoky quartz matrix contains the future jewel in all its developing steps.
   (b) The cover sentence of the program plan is sufficiently broad to cover the facts that will be developed from it. (It is helpful to think of these facts as <u>details</u> that could be counted, rather than as abstractions.)

2. (a) The "rough" taken from the matrix similarly contains the remaining stages of the developing jewel (fewer, of course, than those inherent in the entire matrix).
   (b) Because the three elements of the proof phrase equal the cover sentence's validity, one element of that proof phrase suggests roughly only one-third of the possible details of its predecessor.

3. (a) The preform is appreciably smaller than the chunk from which it was cut. While the chunk might have produced several gems of industrial quality, as a preform its possibilities are considerably limited.
   (b) The explanation step that follows the first element of the proof phrase does not express all details that could conceivably be adduced. It is thus a further development of the narrowing process, from the implication of many details to that of a lessening number.

4. (a) The finished jewel has individual being in time and space; it is the end result.
   (b) The specific example that is cited to "prove" its predecessors has individual being in time and space. It is a particular happening.

Following the steps in which Henry displayed his rubies, our descent from the general cover sentence to the specific example looks like this:

matrix	cover sentence
"rough"	first proof element
preform	its explanation
jewel	specific example

In both situations, of course, the steps represent an approximation. We have compressed the various operations that reduce the gemstone from rough to preform. Similarly, a writer might find it desirable to include another step or two before he cites his specific example. Again, the rockhound might find flaws in the preform that rule out the expense of professional cutting, just as a writer might not care to cite a specific example.

Nevertheless, the requirement of four levels is basic to the effectiveness of our algorithm. Such a planned descent insures adequate exploration of a subject within a paragraph, as you will see. It provides guidelines for the student who has trouble with expansion, just as it calls a halt to the prolific writer who pushes on and on, straying into areas outside his logical boundaries.

Let's look at a simple example of the algorithm in use.

cover sentence   Typing is a useful skill.
    first proof   It sometimes leads to an exciting career.
      explanation   A typist at a show-business firm may step into a vacant slot.
        example   Jane Doe, formerly a typist at KXZR, now sits on the news desk.

In our simple cover sentence, then, the reader is entitled to infer that typing is a useful skill for any of a dozen reasons:

always in demand as a job
easy to learn
helpful in most professions
assures readability in everything you write
involves no stressful responsibility
provides a stepping stone to more glamorous jobs
can be worked at part-time

Even abstractions can be pinned down to countable possibilities. If your subject matter is so generalized, so airy that it seems to have no divisions, chances are you'd better make it more specific to start with.

The second level is the expression of *any one of the proof-phrase elements,* and thus a reduction to no more than one-third of the meanings implied by the cover sentence. (They equal its validity.)

The third level is an *explanation* of that one proof-phrase element. Whatever you write about it will not constitute everything that might conceivably be said. You therefore subtract still further from the number of possible meanings.

The fourth level is the specific example, which desirably suggests no further development. Most often it conveys uniqueness: one of a kind, one time, one place, one person, one happening.

In all levels except (usually) the specific example, the kinds of sentences produced by the algorithm raise questions (or expectations) in the reader's mind. The succeeding sentence should respond to that expectation. Let's see what might develop from the simple sentences about typing.

STATEMENT	YOUR QUESTION
Typing is a useful skill (for three reasons).	Why? To me, sitting at a typewriter all day seems like a dead end.
It sometimes leads to an exciting career.	How do you mean? (Maybe we disagree on the meaning of *exciting!*)
A typist at a show business firm may step into a vacant slot.	Show me! I've heard claims like that before.
Jane Doe, formerly a typist at KXZR, now sits on the news desk.	Okay. Your mention of a particular person who did just that convinces me.

The simple order to follow, then, is to originate a sentence to which the proof phrase is added or suggested. Next, you state one of the proofs, following that with an explanation. Finally, you complete the requirements of the algorithm with a specific example.

Thus, our algorithm is very simple, despite its Arabic name. *Algorithm* suggests something mystic, like Aladdin's genie. The new clarity of written thought it affords you may indeed seem magical.

Let's look at other examples.

1.	*Cover statement*	In addition to a good income, most of us expect a satisfactory career to deliver at least three benefits.
	One benefit	For one thing, we want it to represent a continuing challenge.
	Explanation	A healthy person's natural self-esteem invites the interplay of his personal resources.
	Specific example	The successful executive's favorite relaxation, for example, is likely to be a competitive sport like golf or tennis.
2.	*Cover statement*	With so many teenagers cutting school to play Pac-Man, nervous operators of arcade computer games are seeking various strategies to avoid community reprisal.
	One strategy	One California arcade owner has devised an ingenious scheme.
	Explanation	He manages not only to soothe parents' concern about missed classes, but also their annoyance about wasted allowances.
	Specific example	To every youngster who presents monthly evidence of perfect attendance at school, he awards free-game tokens.
3.	*Cover statement*	The popularity of video games is based on several innately human qualities.
	One quality	Chief of these is the male animal's need to protect what is his.
	Explanation	Typically, video games call on the player to defend himself or his troops against attack by an invader, usually from outer space, whom the odds strongly favor.

Example	Thus, in playing Defenders, Missile Command, Asteroids, Space Invaders, and the like, the young males who flock to the arcades are recapping untold eons of fighting off cave bears, hungry wolves, raiding barbarians, slave-traders, pirates.
4. *Cover statement*	The amount of money and credit available in the country at any time is determined in various ways, referred to as M-1, M-2, and M-3.
One way	The Federal Reserve Bank, charged with regulation of the money supply, focuses most often on M-1.
Explanation	M-1 determines the amount of currency in circulation, as well as the deposits in all kinds of checking accounts.
Example	These are the funds most readily available to the public for day-to-day spending.

Such a set of thoughts as these proves very useful without further expansion. It can serve as an introduction to the 500-word paper so often assigned in college. Reversed, it patterns an excellent conclusion, as you will see later. And, of course, its sentences can form an internal paragraph in any sort of longer work.

All this may seem very simple to you. Unless yours is a disciplined mind, however, you are likely to find it difficult to pluck out of the blue four sentences that descend in levels of generality. The more lively your thinking, the more possibilities for exploration that bob up to offer themselves. As in the children's game of Gossip, at the end you may find your example at a tangent from your general thought.

Here is a fact that will surprise you.

Students generally find it far easier to produce the algorithm's first two steps from a *program plan* cover sentence suggesting *three* proofs than to effect a similar descent from a random sentence.

The requirement that adds the proof phrase to your general statement is a genuine short-cut to the logical development of thought. By the time you have practiced our algorithm a number of times, you will find that not only have you clarified your writing, but also your thought processes.

But how do we enlarge that algorithm into a full-length paper? You'll find that principle detailed in our next chapter.

SUMMARY

The *cover sentence* consists of a subject, a focus on that subject, and a *proof phrase* that suggests the three main divisions of your discussion. (The *proof phrase* may be implied rather than stated.)

Such a sentence by its versatility will generate either of the two basic kinds of communication: (a) informational or analytical, and (b) justificative or persuasive.

The cover sentence directs the writer's discussion in hierarchical or *top-down* order, from the most general thought to the most specific. This order has long proved to convey information with maximum clarity.

The desirability of top-down order, traditional in textbooks, has been validated recently by recent developments in artificial intelligence. Scientific studies with computers far more advanced than those in industry suggest that, like them, the human brain handles information in hierarchical levels of difficulty. Such rising responsibility corresponds to the chain of command typical of the military and most corporations.

The desirable top-down order in writing is mapped by an *algorithm* (a set of steps) that guides the exploration of a thought from the cover sentence to a specific example—from the concept that covers the highest number of potential details to that which offers the fewest. In its narrowing descent of countable possibilities, the algorithm parallels the process by which raw material undergoes a process that eventually limits it to the single finished product.

For the average writer, such a logical development of thought ordinarily proves difficult. With the short-cut provided by the *program plan,* however, that logic is simplified into *cover sentence, first proof, explanation,* and *specific example.* Thus, the algorithm provides dependable aid to the clarification of thought, both for writer and for reader.

ASSIGNMENTS

1. Think of some simple process that reduces a raw product to a specific article, such as a jewel. Write out the various steps by which its potential for other uses is gradually diminished. (A newly sheared fleece offers good possibilities.)

2. Devise a cover sentence that states your chief reason for improving your writing skills. Then work out the descent to a specific example.

3. Study the following examples reprinted from various sources. In each, try to ascertain the logical relation that each step bears to its predecessor. Underline the words in each sentence that carry forward the meaning. Ask yourself how you know that a narrowing of thought takes place.

A.   (1) The men of this [Mesolithic] period spread over a wider area than their paleolithic predecessors, who seem to have been confined to England and Wales. (2) They lived both in caves and in the open. (3) One type of home occupied by those who did not live in caves was the pit-dwelling, (4) which was built by digging a circular hole in the earth, throwing up the excavated earth around the hole, and covering the top with poles and branches or skins.[5]

B.   (1) Most of the new employees [at GE's microelectronics center] will work in a futuristic "clean room" that houses the manufacturing process and is the heart of the microelectronics facility. (2) In that 25,000-square-foot sealed area, workers cloaked in spotless white nylon coveralls, hoods, boots, and gloves work amid gleaming steel machinery and glass walls. (3) The nylon suits—called "bunny suits" by the workers—are not for the protection of the employees, but for the protection of the chips made at the center. (4) A stray whisker or even a hint of perspiration on a fingertip can ruin the silicon chips' electric circuits, so tiny that they can be seen only with a powerful microscope.[6]

Thom Hill

C.   (1) But before [English teachers] turn all remedial instruction over to computers, there are two attributes of this approach which we should look at more closely. (2) The first attribute is the sequencing of frames. (3) Implicit in the design of drill and practice programs is the logical ordering of the information presented to the students. (4) Each frame should help establish the basic knowledge needed to negotiate the next frame and reinforce the learning of the previous one.[7]

William Wresch

D.   Long before Christianity, *three* was a holy number, wrote Sigmund Freud. Probably he had in mind, not the myths and rituals of the Hindus, but those of civilizations more directly affecting European thought. Among the most ancient were the Babylonians of the Bible, who assigned the great divisions of the cosmos to two successive triads. First came the primitive "universal" gods, those responsible for the heavens, the earth, and the watery elements. Later in history came the triad representing natural forces: the sun, the moon, and fertility. The latter was Ishtar, the Biblical Astoreth and Phoenician Astarte. In Europe, the conquering Celts left traces of their religion in which *three* was compellingly sacred. Their statuary often represents their gods with three heads or in triplicate, to emphasize their importance. During the period in which the Celts worshipped female rather than male divinities, a triad of mother goddesses insured fruitfulnesses and abundance. In Freud's mind, however, it was probably the pantheon of the Greeks whose triads most affected European thought, still strongly evident in our folklore and superstitions. A German scholar at the beginning of this century located more than 120 triads important to Greek culture. Centuries earlier, scholars of the Renaissance, poring over the rediscovered Greek manuscrips, associated the many triads with the Christian Trinity, assessing them as a unity comprised of three component parts.

NOTES

1. Russell A. Hunt, "Toward a Process-Intervention Model in Literature Teaching," *College English*, 44, no. 4, (April 1982), p. 345.

2. Hunt, p. 345.

3. George Edgin Pugh, *The Biological Origin of Human Values* (New York: Basic Books, 1977), p. 96.

4. Pugh, p. 37.

5. *History of England* (New York: Harper & Row, 1957), p. 12.

6. "GE Has Big Plans for Microelectronics," *The News & Observer of Raleigh* (Raleigh, N.C.), p. 10D.

7. William Wresch, "Computers in English Class: Finally Beyond Grammar and Spelling Drills," *College English*, 44, no. 5 (September 1982), 484.

2
STRUCTURING THE PARAGRAPH: A SPECIAL PATTERN

GOAL: To devise a structure tree and write a paragraph

You will remember from our last chaper that we form patterns—gestalt configurations or "wholes"—of everything we perceive, ranging from the sound of a siren to the sentences you are reading.

Most of our behavior patterns are created on a conscious level and then transferred to automatic or subconscious control. As small children, we laboriously learn to tell time or to tie a bowknot—and then never give those actions another thought. We memorize the keyboard of a typewriter or piano and thereafter store its arrangement in our subconscious. We spend weeks in a driver's training course, whereupon we respond automatically to road conditions and traffic while our mind strays elsewhere.

Creative problem-solving calls for the disassembling of such patterns and then a different restructuring.

In a certain engineering corporation, for example, prospective employees are tested for their abilities to break long-established patterns. One problem asks the engineers to remove a pingpong ball from the bottom of a narrow four-inch cylinder—without touching either object. So far, no one has been successful. The solution requires a very simple but indecorous act.

Even when randomness is essential, when just to *suggest* a pattern risks enormous disaster, the human brain seeks gestalts.

In World War II, for example, the hard-pressed British sought—and found—a pattern in the "unbreakable" German code they dubbed Enigma. The officer in charge of Britain's Air Intelligence, Peter Calvocaressi, writes:

The basic problem in cryptography is to get randomness. Left to themselves human beings, and machines operated by human beings, quickly stop being purely random and fall into some pattern or other. At one point the German cryptographers responsible for finding entirely random settings for an Enigma cypher thought they had hit on a bright solution. Every day the concentration camps rendered returns giving the numbers of prisoners who had been delivered to the camp that day, the number who had died or been killed, and the number of surviving inmates at the end of the day. These were truly random figures. They were reported in a medium-grade cypher and the recipients passed them on to their Enigma colleagues who used them in determining the settings of a particular Enigma cypher. [British Intelligence] was reading that medium-grade cypher and it realized too that these daily concentration camp returns were being used in Enigma. So these sad, grisly statistics of human suffering and indignity played a part which the piteous victims never dreamed of.[1]

Pugh explains the human need to form configurations as "an important way of conserving cybernetic [governing] resources at the critical decision level."[2] To be random expends costly psychic energy. Our subconscious fairly thirsts for order.

It follows, then, that anyone who writes to any extent will settle into some kind of pattern—even if only to put down whatever blips on his mental screen. Since a means of achieving a highly practical pattern for writing is available, it seems logical to acquire its benefits.

THE PLAN FOR THE PARAGRAPH: THE STRUCTURE TREE

A skill like driving a car or typing is practiced until it becomes automatic, combining physical action and mental processes.

For that reason, we urge you to plan even simple practice paragraphs *on paper.* As we move through simple stages into those that are more complex, it will be tempting to keep your plan for a short paper in your head. Resist the easy way now, however, and you will gain considerable benefits later.

Well, how do we go about this essential planning? How do we expand the algorithm into a paragraph or paper?

No doubt you've already guessed. Instead of coming down the four steps so that we finish with four sentences, we repeat any of the steps according to the optimal division of our material.

(The definition of the algorithm permits recursiveness, you recall.)

Consider our typical sentence with its suggestion of three proofs. Clearly, we shall need to produce three sentences on that second level instead of one.

Moreover, we must provide each one of those three proof statements with its own explanation and its specific example. (Perhaps it may require several sentences of explanation and several examples!) Of course, we finish with each one of the three proof sections before tackling the next.

To reflect our planning for these additional explanations and examples, let's turn to a simple device far more agreeable to use than the formal outline—the structure tree. Such trees have been around for sometime, although not in composition classes. Because computer programmers utilize them in breaking down their complex problems, however, we began to appreciate their possibilities. In contrast to the rigid, list-like outline, trees reveal relationships at a glance, even when roughly scrawled as a work plan. Moreover, changes become simply a matter of drawing in a new branch or scratching out an old one.

We reproduce a simple tree chart that IBM's Marian Bohl includes in her book, *A Guide for Programmers*. (See Bohl's Structure Chart below.) "We identify first the major function to be accomplished, then its subfunctions, their subfunctions, and so on," she writes. In such diagrams,

the logical structure of the design should practically jump off the structure chart page.[3]

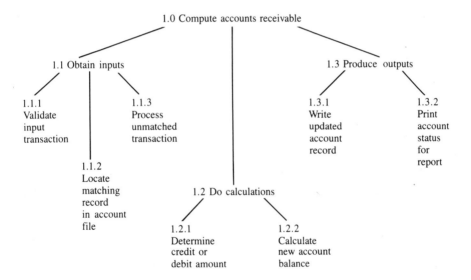

As you consider Bohl's top-down chart, you'll note that the problem in its entirety is to *compute accounts receivable*. (For example, a department store wants to determine the amounts owed it by its charge customers.)

The next block down on your left indicates the first step in arriving at these sums: *obtaining inputs,* perhaps the charge slips. Because this is only one of three logical divisions of that particular task, it naturally requires fewer operations than the task itself.

On the bottom level, you see that obtaining inputs has in turn been partitioned. Again, the block to your left, *validate input transaction,* certainly is not equal in tasks to the entire process of obtaining inputs.

Presumably, if we wished to provide an example of validating those inputs, we should represent only part of a whole, for clearly more than one example could be cited.

What we have, then, is the numerical reduction required by our algorithm. The tree design is fully appropriate for our uses. (See Our Structure Chart below.) To demonstrate, we reproduce Bohl's tree divisions, filling in the spaces with the supports required by the following cover sentence:

Ideally, a job should be more than a way to pay bills.

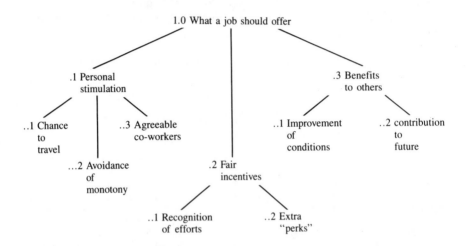

Let's come down the middle this time. As one of three main supports, a job should provide *fair incentives*. Of those incentives, nothing is more important than *recognition of an employee's efforts*.

Again—at the far right, a given individual wishes that his or her work will *contribute to the good of others*. Perhaps that good may have *some lasting effect* in the overall scheme of things.

As we traced the steps of the algorithm in this chart, were you aware that the omission of examples robs the points of the full impact they might have? Presumably, lack of space limited Bohl's development. But, as you can see, that additional lowest level is necessary for a full understanding of the topic we choose.

Remember, also, that the number of divisions on any one level may vary. You may have only two main points, or as many as four. Similarly, each main point should be divided according to the available material—not according to the partitioning shown in the illustration. And the example becomes a matter of how deeply you delve into your subject; it may appear on the third level down rather than the fourth.

For the tree diagram of a short paper, notation seems unnecessary. For purposes of designation, however, we simplify Bohl's mathematical notation. The cover sentence is represented by a whole number (1.0). The main points become .1, .2, and .3. At the explanation level we ignore tradition altogether and use *two* preceding decimals. For the fourth level, examples, we write Ex. Surely, no notation could be simpler, yet adequately serve the purpose! (We do present formal notation later, however.)

PLAN INTO PARAGRAPH

In the last chapter, we illustrated the algorithm's four steps by an analogous process: the development of a ruby from its spawning bed in quartz to the finished jewel.

Let us return to our rockhound friend Henry to continue the analogy. Henry, you remember, is laying out the best of his collection of American gemstones for a museum exhibit. Against the gold-foil floor of the case, he has planned a three-striped fan of rubies, sapphires, and emeralds.

At the top, you recall, he has centered the smoky quartz caddy that represents the natural matrix. We left him just after he had laid out the left-hand wedge of rubies, raying them forward in the stages of their processing. Now he is ready for the central wedge of sapphires.

With a smile on his lean, tanned face, Henry centers his favorite rough in front of the matrix. Only a rockhound would give it a second glance—this dull, brownish lump that resembles half an unprepossessing potato. Yet it is remarkable indeed—it has cradled not only a star sapphire—but also a star ruby!

Next, he sets out a clustered rainbow of sapphire preforms—knoblets and ovoids and disks of violet, cornflower blue, green, yellow, almost-orange. Now for the finished brilliants in various cuts, glinting with colored lights ... He decides to frame them around the two best stones, two deep blue cabochons big as large grapes, their six-rayed stars perfectly centered.

The emeralds for the right-hand stick will suffer in comparison, he knows. They are fewer in number and less desirable in quality. But how often are flawless emeralds found anywhere? The rough is unusual, though—a six-sided grass-green finger edged in a fringe of its natural setting, white limestone.

Beyond it he places his few lush preforms like rectangular buttons, feeling them velvety cool to the touch. Their color is good; not watery, but a deep, true green.

He finishes the design with a scattering of ring-sized stones in the traditional emerald cut and stands back to view the results. Refracting the spotlight he has arranged, the three-striped fan quivers with glinting light—red and yellow and blue and green.

Remembering the personal experience involved with each gem, Henry allows himself a smile of pride. Let Amsterdam keep its glittering hoards. Rockhounding pays more desirable dividends!

As you have realized, Henry's exhibit is a tangible representation of the algorithm's recursiveness, its permissible repetition of certain steps.

Just as Henry progressed downward from the matrix (the container) to follow each gem through its chronological processes, you will develop each main point through its explanation and specific examples before continuing to the next. Each main point introduces a top-down process that you take up in turn.

Your progress in individual steps is always downward; you fairly leap to the top of the next branch before descending again. In an old musical, Fred Astaire performs an analogous dance on a short flight of stairs. In white tie and tails, he appears at the top where, to the beat of the music, he taps out a brief patent leather tattoo. Then nimbly he drums his way down, pausing on each step to patter out a separate brief routine. Descended, with a graceful leap he's at the top again, repeating the smooth downward flow. Like gravity, his dance is one-directional, never an upward climb, but a dashing swoop.

You could actually play a tune like "Frère Jacques" to the pattern of the structure tree, beginning with a three-note chord as the cover sentence!

Here is a simple structure tree and the paragraph it produces:

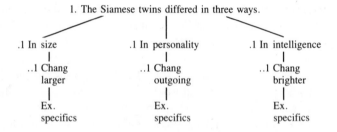

1.0 Although irrevocably joined by flesh, the Siamese twins differed in major aspects.
   .1 They differed in size.
      ..1 Chang was physically the more robust.
        Ex.   He was three inches taller as well as stockier than the stunted Eng.
   .2 The twins also differed in personality.
      ..1 Chang, the more outgoing, dominated his glum, morose brother.
        Ex.   Their families report harsh, bitter arguments that would have separated two ordinary men.
   .3 They differed, too, in intelligence.
      ..1 Chang's good head for business allowed them to retire as well-to-do.
        Ex.   They bought large farms in North Carolina and paid for their wives with gold.

The following tree shows repetition on the explanation level.

1.0 Americans are fascinated with English royalty for three reasons.
   .1 For one thing, we love the age-old ritual and pageantry, missing from our own tradition.
      ..1 In one July week in 1981, an estimated 55 million Americans enjoyed England's royal wedding, televised by the networks at a cost of $5 million.

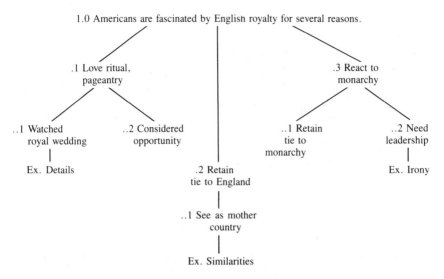

1.0 Americans are fascinated by English royalty for several reasons.

.1 Love ritual, pageantry

..1 Watched royal wedding

Ex. Details

..2 Considered opportunity

.2 Retain tie to England

..1 See as mother country

Ex. Similarities

.3 React to monarchy

..1 Retain tie to monarchy

..2 Need leadership

Ex. Irony

    Ex. The glittering splendor of the cathedral and its ceremony, the golden coaches and shiny horses, the red-coated soldiers in their tall black busbies—all proved irresistible to people who celebrate a Puritan ancestry.

  ..2 Many Americans considered the display to be a cultural opportunity unlikely to be repeated.

 .2 Our great interest in English royalty may also result from daily reminders of our English heritage.

  ..1 As children, many of us heard our teachers call England the mother country.

    Ex. Not only have we inherited its language, customs, and laws, but our concept of democracy flowered from English freedoms, as history demonstrates.

 .3 Psychologically, Americans' response to England's benign monarchy may be instinctive.

  ..1 Such a reaction may somehow be inherited, for until World War I, virtually all immigrants had lived under a monarchical government.

  ..2 On an even deeper level, far more of us are followers than are leaders; the homage and respect accorded the monarch symbolize the leadership we seek.

    Ex. Ironically, as our ancestors followed their king into battle, so many Americans continue to follow royalty today—into hairstyles and fashions.

This kind of paragraph (actually a miniature paper) will serve as an economical practice form for the kinds of development we shall be demonstrating henceforth.

DETERMINING A FOCUS AND ITS BOUNDARIES

Usually, you decide on your general subject (or have it assigned to you) and then work out one particular aspect to cover.

For example, if you parallel your subject's many facts to people at a large family reunion, you might decide to focus your camera on a representative from each of the four generations present—your great-grandmother, your grandmother, your mother, and your sister. From many possibilities (all the members from Topeka; all those with red hair; all the children, etc.), these four constitute the focus in your view-finder.

But you will not always work in subject-focus order.

Sometimes, with the program plan's proof phrase in mind, you may stumble into three elements in your reading that a writer has presented subconsciously, or that represent logical divisions of the subject. Whatever links them together becomes your subject, ready-made.

Most often, deciding on a focus is a matter of pondering the possibilities, a complicated process that we shall not try to describe. It is often helpful, you'll find, to apply the questions inherent in the cover sentence's proof phrase:

	because of three facts (*Why?*)
	through three examples (*How?*)
So-and-so	as three types (*Which?*)
is	with three characteristics (*What?*)
such-and-such	in three areas (*Where?*)
	in three time-periods (*When?*)

These are the familiar reporter's questions, possessing the potential of sorting out facts. They not only help you to arrive at a topic, but also to support it.

If you are writing practice paragraphs, you may simply choose a subject with which you are thoroughly familiar and preface it with these WH-question words. We'll choose two subjects at random, *vans* and *dieting*.

Why buy a van?	*Why* diet? (doctor's advice? self-image?)
Where buy a van?	*Where* diet? (fat farm? special camp?)
Which van should you buy?	*Which* diet should you undertake?
When should you buy a van?	*When* should you diet? (at exam time?)
How much should you pay?	*How long* should you diet?

Perhaps the most troublesome decision to make about the focus of your topic is to set its limitations. How much is enough for a practice paragraph—and how specific must you be?

Such questions are not easily answered. In general, you should not skim off the top of a voluminous subject. The three basic causes of the Russian Revolution are not to be condensed into a paragraph! Instead, you delve deeply into a minor division (the fate of the Czar's family) and retrieve a topic to which ten sentences or so can do justice: three reasons for believing a certain claimant is the Princess Anastasia.

Let's take an example. Suppose you are the founder and leader of a small hard-rock music group. You've had several years' experience in the various complications of getting such a group underway: choosing members, managing rehearsals, lining up gigs, getting publicity. You are well aware that you'll have to single out a certain section of your material. Aha, you decide, I'll write about how a beginning group goes about developing a distinctive sound!

Wisely, you start off making notes. I'll give the Beatles as an example, you think; everybody knows *them*. Then I'll mention the kinds of sounds there are, and how you should settle on one sound and not waver back and forth. And how you can make special use of what talent you have available, some way-out instrument, maybe, or some guy who can sing. And where rhythms fit into the picture ...

About there, you pause, none too happily. All that special know-how cannot possibly fit into one paragraph, if you're to do your material justice. You *can* cut the topic down to just one distinctive sound, but do you really want to? You hate to waste all those good facts by such a drastic limitation.

Instead, you say to yourself, I'll put these notes aside for a full-length paper. And to write this paragraph, I'll stick to a few strategies for auditioning new members for the group ...

The basis for your choice of topic, then, is determined by its intrinsic requirements, its *breadth*—not by the amount of information you have available. This is relative, of course. Presumably the officials of the ACC could write several printed pages on the new ruling, just as a scientist could write a long article on the effects of a greenhouse in heating a building. For you, a paragraph on either one would be enough.

In certain situations, you are entitled to your opinion on a subject, even though you lack basic facts and figures. You do not necessarily have to produce statistics to justify your attitude toward the new state tax, a political figure, the educational system, and so on.

Here are some examples of pruning a large subject into a size commensurate with a programmed paragraph:

FULL LENGTH PAPER	PROGRAMMED PARAGRAPH
The effects of three major factors in brainwashing	The causes for a captive's feeling of dependency
The arguments against genetic tailoring	The desirability of choosing the sex of your child
The fashioning of a political image	The factor of benevolence ascribed to a certain politico
Revolutionary developments in photographic equipment	Some advantages of the 35 mm single-lens reflex camera
The factors involved in slapstick humor	What's funny about skidding on a banana peel?
The problems of extended life expectancy in the Western world	Who wants to be 100?
The importance of news in the hierarchy of network programming	The chief requirements of an anchorman

If you consider your material carefully, you'll have no trouble in similarly limiting your topic.

THE "DIVISIONS OF MAN" PATTERN

You are now ready to benefit from a remarkable pattern that considerably simplifies a wide variety of writing, both in the academic world and in your professional life. We call it a *template*—a ready-made design that brings order to what may be a wide variety of available facts. With some imagination, you can see its parallel in the manufacture of microelectronic chips.

One of the critical steps in creating a batch of chips involves reproducing a computer-designed pattern of tiny channels in each micron-thin layer of silicon. As one layer after another is applied to the crystal of pure silicon, a pattern for its particular set of minute roadways is photographed on it. Then acid eats away the areas exposed to light, leaving tiny, properly patterned channels for conductive metal.

To expose the proper areas, the chips are repeatedly photographed through a series of *photo masks*. A mask is a flat piece of glass overlaid with a thin chromium plate, cut like a stencil in the required design. If these masks were larger, they could be thought of as *templates*.

> *template:* A pattern or gauge, such as a thin metal
> plate with a cut pattern, used as a guide
> in making something accurately.
>
> *American Heritage Dictionary*

The intangible templates that we provide in this book are three-fold patterns with which you overlay your material. They enable you to determine accurately certain essential aspects of it. They provide you with the divisions of the critical proof phrase.

Suppose, for example, you are writing copy for an ad agency. Your assignment calls for what amounts to a paragraph on the benefits to the buyer of a certain sports car.

It would help to have a reliable pattern for organizing the facts you possess.

Or suppose that you are a student in a required English literature course. You must write a brief study of Othello's character. Your general impression is that he's jealous; you can't remember any other characteristic that distinguishes him.

With the divisions supplied by this chapter's template, however, you know what to look for as you glance through the play. While other students are coming up with main points that are simply synonyms for jealousy, you utilize an admirable pattern that divides the whole man—the framework for everything that can possibly be said.

THE MOST USEFUL TOPIC FOR WRITING

"The proper study of mankind is man," wrote Alexander Pope in a much-quoted phrase. Certainly humanity, singular or plural, furnishes a never-ending source of subject-matter on which to write. You may expound on nuclear fission, cybernetics, solar energy, or theology, but your underlying concern lies in the possibilities whereby these arcane subjects may eventually affect man. We continue to live in a man-centered universe.

As a subject for study, man is divided by philosophers into a limited number of parts. Some of these are two-part divisions, diads:

body and soul
flesh and spirit
male and female
yang and yin

More, however, are triads, as you will see. These in turn fall into two classes: (1.) those that group together what is visible and tangible about man with what is not; and (2.) those that exclude the physical in order to classify what is as real but unseen. After explaining the two groups, we shall discuss their potential usefulness to you in a wide range of your future writing requirements.

We shall simply take the simplest of the triads and explore its possibilities; you can mix or match the interpretations as you choose, or as your subject matter may require. That triad is the familiar body-mind-spirit.

Body can be thought of as everything physical or apparent to the eye: how the individual looks—size, coloring, clothing, stance, gestures; or what the body can do—its capabilities in sports, for example. In a paper that builds from what is considered least important to what is most important, *body* becomes the first main point. Philosophers consider it the least weighty (!) of the three, yet it is that physical aspect of which we are first aware in meeting someone. In an essay, a few words about *body* provide an image for the reader, a picture in the mind, to which we can attribute the various abstractions we shall introduce.

The second of the triad, the *mind,* also enjoys a broad interpretation. It can be thought of as any intellectual activity that is rational and logical. *Mind* as a cause may be extended to cover the intellectual accomplishments of a person that result from it, such as his education and career. The concern of *mind* is that mental activity distinguishable from what we customarily label *feelings*.

The concept of such feelings, *spirit,* is broader still. At base, an individual's spirit is rooted in emotions, a cluster of responses that we sum up as personality. Whether it is more or less important than *mind* is a choice you make as writer, depending on your personal values.

These divisions crop up constantly. In an article in *Time* about the appointment of the first woman Supreme Court justice, Hugh Sidey wrote:

> Dozens of Ronald Reagan's aides, acting more like clinical psychologists than bureaucrats, probed her [Sandra O'Connor's] shadings of emotion, her intellect, her theology.[4]

A current magazine appraises its readers in terms of their age and sex, their social rank, and their intellectual interests.

A casual reference to the financier Hetty Green may refer to these divisions with no intent to develop them: "When she was still a gangling teen-ager, shy and introspective, she determined to conquer Wall Street."

The second of the two classes of triads ignores the body in order to section the intangible. In this class, there are three that are more or less familiar to you: The oldest is Aristotle's pathos, ethos, and logos (the emotional, the spiritual, and the intellectual), the factors in accomplishing persuasion, set forth in his *Rhetoric,* written between 322–320 B.C. While this is the oldest of the three, it is as contemporary as the appeal for CARE in the current issue of some popular magazine, as we'll see in a later chapter. It is likely that every important political speech ever made is based on Aristotle's triad, whether or not the speaker knows of its origin. In its introduction the speech will snare the audience's emotions by some human interest story that will arouse pity or fear. It will establish the credibility of the speaker, assuring the audience of his integrity and the trust they may place in his message to bear out some arguments that sound unarguably logical and reasonable.

The next triad is much closer to us in time.

Few readers will not have heard of Sigmund Freud's psychic states, the id, ego, and superego.

id	the instinctual impulses and demands for immediate satisfaction of primitive needs
ego	the conscious component that most immediately controls behavior and is most in touch with external reality
superego	the incorporation of the perceived moral standards of the community; it includes the conscience

This grouping is the least useful of the triads as a means of organizing a profile or character study, because it rests on psychoanalysis. Professional writers of fiction or drama often set up a trio of characters each of whom embodies or represents one of these states.

The most recent of the major groups is that of transactional analysis, a division of the ego states analyzed by Eric Berne, author of *Games People Play* (1964). This triad offers excellent possibilities for a variety of uses. In a later book, *What Do You Say After You Say Hello?* the author describes the divisions of Parent, Adult, and Child in a programmed paragraph (divided here for easier reading):

> The basic interest of transactional analysis is the study of ego states, which are coherent systems of thought and feeling manifested by corresponding patterns of behavior. Each human being exhibits three types of ego states. The first,

colloquially called the Parent, is derived from parental figures. In this state, he feels, thinks, acts, talks, and responds just as one of his parents did when he was little. This ego state is active, for example, in raising his own children. Even when he is not actually exhibiting this ego state, it influences his behavior as the "Parental influence," performing the functions of a conscience.

In the second ego state, the Adult, he appraises his environment objectively and calculates its possibilities and probabilities on the basis of past experience. The Adult functions like a computer.

Each person carries within a little boy or girl, who feels, thinks, acts, talks, and responds just the way he or she did when he or she was a child of a certain age. This ego state is called the Child. The Child is not regarded as "childish" or "immature," which are Parental words, but as childlike, meaning like a child of a certain age, and the important factor here is the age, which may be anywhere between two and five years in ordinary circumstances. It is important for the individual to understand his Child, not only because it is going to be with him all his life, but because it is the most valuable part of his personality.[5]

As you can understand, an analysis in which you find one of these last three classes represented in the object of your study suggests a weightier treatment than if you simply divide the qualities of some real-life person or literary character into appearance, personality, and intellect. To show you the possibilities of the latter group, however, we shall generate a programmed paragraph of such an analysis later in this chapter.

SOME SUGGESTED USES
OF THE TEMPLATE

In the following examples of the divisions-of-man template, you will find a variety of possibilities from which you may derive your own topics for various kinds of communication. We list them without classification, some partially developed, others simply cover sentences.

1. In "Silicone Valley" several large corporations supply prized employees with extra perks in the form of a well-equipped gymnasium, advanced study programs, and a clubhouse for drinking and dancing.
2. Our concept of the levels of deity suggests three specialized areas of power: the awe-inspiring divinity that controls the great forces of nature and the overall destiny of mankind; the divinity in human form that assumes some of the limitations of that form; and the divinity as spirit within man, the spark of something greater than the individual, which can only counsel and motivate.
3. Abused children suffer damage on three levels.
4. Polo demands the forces of the entire man—physical, emotional, and intellectual.
5. At that period, the best critics believed that a good novel should stir the emotions, challenge the intellect, and establish some kind of moral stand.
6. Each of the chief characters in *Star Trek* represents one phase of the emotion-logic-intuition triad; to show that man is holistic, the ship's captain embodies a mixture of all three.

7. The attitudes of the food-oriented person toward dieting manifest Berne's three ego states.
8. *Mademoiselle* is directed toward women within a certain range of age, education, and interests.
9. Friendship between men and women functions on three planes.
10. Sports cars built with a third middle seat offer three benefits to the driver: space for an additional passenger, improved judgment of space, and an aesthetic feeling of lateral symmetry.

The divisions of this template—or synonyms for them—may constitute your main points in any paper you write that assesses a particular person. In long articles, you would extend these to allied factors: the individual's heredity and environment—his family and friends, goals, idiosyncracies, hobbies.

A Final Note

We close this chapter with a gentle reminder.

The great weakness common to all non-professional writers—from high school student to major general—is lack of planning *on paper*.

As authority for this statement, we cite David W. Ewing, Executive Editor–Planning of the *Harvard Business Review* and a member of the faculty of the Harvard Business School. In his book *Writing for Results* (1974), he produces and analyzes examples of written communication of the nation's notables, including that of two generals. He demonstrates how more careful preparation might have prevented the given writer's later embarrassment, or even affected the outcome of some important decision.

We quote from Ewing's chapter on "Organizing Facts and Ideas":

> Most good business and professional writers generally would agree, I think, that all but the most unusual men and women need to make notes on paper in planning an important, non-routine communication. Mental notes are not enough.

SUMMARY

Unlike the inhibiting restrictions of the formal outline, the simpler tree diagram encourages beginning writers to plan their work on paper. Because it is open-ended, it allows last-minute changes, deletions and additions. Its familiar design manifests at a glance the logical relations between the various levels of thought. Notation, if necessary, is similarly simplified.

The soundness of the tree diagram is evident in its application to the development of thought or structure in other disciplines. Thus it demonstrates the processing of raw material like the gemstones, in which available choices are comparably decreased to a specific example.

In solving the problem of subject-matter on which to write, students can rely on a template, a writing device that enables him or her to look for facts that fit into each of its divisions. Since almost every subject eventually involves human reactions, the Divisions of Man template is remarkably versatile. It is important to consider the desirable focus on a given subject, slanting or limiting it by asking questions and applying judgment.

ASSIGNMENTS

1. In learning to organize your material, it is remarkably helpful to analyze the writing of others. Thus you will benefit by mapping the structure trees of the following paragraphs. Though C consists of several paragraphs, its tree will follow the same pattern as the shorter work.

A.   The divisions of a newspaper's reading material may be paralleled to Eric Berne's ego states. Its editorial stance suggests the Parent—the admonitory eye that sees clearly through political mists and devious attacks on public funds. Its reporters represent the Adult state. Ideally, they channel "hard" news to the public without fear or favor, seeking out the facts and presenting them straightforwardly. The lighter sections approximate Berne's Child. These are the sports sections, individual self-help columns, comic strips, puzzles.

B.   A career to which you offer years of your life should satisfy Berne's three ego-states. It should generate pleasure and occasional excitement, even fun. It should challenge you intellectually and provide adequate remuneration for your ideas. And it should allow you to feel that you accomplish something for the good of your community, that you are upholding your corner of the world and perhaps even improving it.

C.   Memo from the regional sales manager to the national sales manager of Sure-Tight Cartons, Inc.:

Dear Bob:

I appreciate your questions about Zellit. I've put off mentioning him to you because I knew you really cared about the guy. He's simply burned out and I'm not sure what we ought to do.

You'd be shocked to see how he's let himself go physically. He's flabby and overweight. Clearly he's not exerting the effort to make the calls he should; he drives to a town and then sits in a motel and phones his accounts instead of seeing them in person. I got a complaint on this from Ed Davis of Pine Hill Dairies and a hint about it from Glen Steele of Mayberry.

He has gone soft in the head, too. Lately, his orders—what few there are of them—show carelessness and inattention to necessary details. He's responsible for our billing Kato in D.C. for two carloads of salad containers instead of billing Kato in Richmond. He says he misread the inventory sheets at Purity and ordered them a carload of quarts they don't need and can't store. He let Seabreeze run completely out of half-gallons.

The real problem seems to be deeper than body and mind. He's hurting somewhere unreachable. He's simply not with the job in spirit ... The life's gone out of him; it's not just a matter of tired blood. You wouldn't recognize the guy; his grin is gone and he hasn't come up with a joke in months.

Maybe you should see what you can do.

                                                                    Jim

2. Reread the ten examples of the Divisions of Man cover sentences provided in the section that suggests its various applications. Decide which ones can be covered in a program plan paragraph and which would require a longer discussion.

Of those that you mark as paragraph-size, choose one, develop a tree, and write the paragraph, using details that you consider appropriate.

3. Consider the person who reads what you write—your teacher or employer. Then decide on one of the interpretations of the Divisions of Man possibilities presented earlier in this chapter. Prepare a tree and write a paragraph.

NOTES

1. Peter Calvocaressi, *Top Secret Ultra* (New York: Random House, 1980), p. 15.

2. George Edgin Pugh, *The Biological Origin of Human Values,* (New York: Basic Books, 1977), p. 15.

3. Marilyn Bohl, *A Guide for Programmers* (Englewood Cliffs, N.J.: Prentice-Hall, 1978), p. 46.

4. Hugh Sidey, "Citadel on a Hill," *Time,* 118, no. 3, July 20, 1981, 19.

5. Eric Berne, *What Do You Say After You Say Hello?* (New York: Grove Press, 1972), pp. 11-12.

3
CLARIFYING
OUR THINKING
PROCESSES

Goal: To learn decision-making processes that are useful in planning and writing

Few writers are so brash as to try to explain the complexities of human thought. We can be sure that the mental activity required in writing, however, involves a continuous process of selection. Selection, in turn, is a matter of forming judgments and decisions.

But what goes on in our minds as they whip through such processes?

You'll find that decision-making involves comparison/contrast, classification, division, definition, cause/result—the devices most of us associate with developing essays, without realizing how great a part they play in thought processes.

In this chapter and the next we shall pick up these relationships in turn and examine them squarely. Instead of the blurred outlines they assume when we draw on them subconsciously, we shall discover the most economical and direct benefits to be derived from them, both in exploring a subject and in developing a topic on paper.

Suppose we demonstrate their involvement in decision-making by referring to the computer—a far less complicated mechanism than our brain.

You remember that the computer's CPU (its processing unit) is analogous to your reader's mind. The programmer's commands direct the computer to perform certain actions, just as your written words seek to lead your reader to concur with your judgments and form the same decisions.

In following the programmer's bidding, then, the computer must make simple decisions:

> Is A greater than B? Yes.

Having made the decision (by comparing numbers), it acts on that judgment in response to a command:

> Then progress to C.

This simple decision-making, with its subsequent action, is a response to the programmer's highly useful IF/THEN—ELSE command, which says to the computer what a teacher might say to a pupil:

> "If this number K is greater than this next number M, *then* you must continue your progress to N. Otherwise (*else*)—*if* it is not so great or simply equal to M—*then* you must turn back to Y (and repeat a series of steps).

Simple enough. But several thought processes are required to obey such a command:

Comparison/Contrast:	Is K greater than M? Yes, K is greater than M.
Classification:	By definition, K must be in a separate category from M.
Cause/Result:	Because K is greater than M, that fact becomes a cause that requires further action—as a result.

As we apply *IF/THEN—ELSE* to more meaningful statements, you will see how such processes figure in more involved decision-making or selection:

> *If* a sea creature nurses its young, *then* it is considered a mammal. Otherwise (*else*) it must be relegated to some other classification.

Clearly, then, classification can be an end result of comparison/contrast, thereby suggesting definition. (Definition includes both classification and differentiation.)

By extension, our natural "train of thought" (a worn-out metaphor) suggests a continuation into cause/result. A given decision usually becomes a cause for subsequent results. As you know, once the public stopped thinking of porpoises as big fish, they began to accord them the consideration given sentient mammals.

> *If* I write the rough draft of my paper by Friday, *then* I can put it aside for the weekend. Otherwise (*else*) I'll have to write the whole thing Monday.

The implied result to the decision to delay goes this way: Because I won't have the necessary time interval in which to gain a fresh perspective of my paper, it may not turn out as well.

In more complicated problem-solving, your reasoning might be represented thus:

> *If* I send the second missionary over with the second cannibal, *then* I must leave him
> and bring back the cannibal. Otherwise *(else),* there will be two cannibals and just
> one missionary left together.

This highly improbable eventuality concerns the much-cited problem of the three
missionaries and three cannibals, all of whom must cross a river in a canoe
holding no more than two at a time. The problem lies in the proviso that the
missionaries must never be outnumbered—on either shore—by the cannibals,
lest they should be eaten.

(You can program a computer to exhaust all possible combinations—or you
can use twigs and acorns.)

Let's examine the components of decision-making in a typical everyday
setting.

Suppose you are driving down a main thoroughfare in your town when, a
block ahead, you spot a small black foreign car. As you close in behind it, you
note an oddity: the car has a fifth wheel! The anomaly is spinning right along,
close to its left rear neighbor, yet somewhat smaller and further forward.

As you overtake the small car to pass it, you recognize its make—a Saab.
Then, in a split second, you glimpse a further surprise—an interior full of shiny
metal housing, and perhaps a gauge or dial.

Now you must give your attention to your driving; you don't get another
good look until you make a right turn, well ahead of this escapee from a James
Bond movie. Across the front of the car, where the bumper ought to be, a sort of
sparse fringe like a skimpy mustache descends to the street. More and more
peculiar! Is the Saab a street sweeper? If so, small as it is, it must be Supercar.

You drive along, your mind firing IF/THEN—ELSE's. Eventually you
decide on the solution. The Saab must be a measuring device, probably
computerized. The extra wheel and the front fringe (sensors, no doubt) suggest
that it provides information about the condition of the road's surface.

At last, you think, some action on those potholes! And you hope your logic
isn't wishful thinking.

Let's consider your most obvious mental activity as you arrived at the
eventual decision.

Your mind automatically registered first the differences between the foreign
car and American makes. Probably this was a matter of superimposing a
composite outline of one on the other (for a millionth of a second), much as is
done by the computerized graphics plotter in a Detroit manufacturer's design
work-station. Later, you evoked the familiar image of a street sweeper as a
contrast to the Saab.

Your various comparisons and contrasts sought to achieve an end: the
"identity" of the strange vehicle. In finding similarities (comparing) you were

trying to *classify,* that is, to find a more general category into which the Saab would fit. In finding differences (contrasting) you were differentiating it from others in a class. Together, as we mentioned earlier, these are the basic factors of a dictionary's definition.

Moreover, your mind was not content to identify the vehicle in terms of what it was; you set out to establish just what purpose might be served by such a measuring device. Again, we see the natural progression to cause/result.

Clearly, processes that constitute so much of our judgment and decision-making are vital tools in the planning of good communication, as well as in the writing process. You may be sure that your reader's mind will also busy itself in similar fashion, as it examines and tests your message.

COMPARISON/CONTRAST

Our language limits us to three ways of describing an object or an action to someone who has never seen it.

1. We can apply adjectives:

> All the seven extremely weary old American computer programmers who participated

2. We can focus on some part of the whole:

> The newest board games are played on a large flat computer screen built into a table. In each corner a rectangular "menu" lists the activities required: throwing dice, drawing cards, making moves, etc. Like the checker at a cafeteria, you simply touch the appropriate item with your finger.

3. We can go beyond the thing to compare it to something else.

> A floppy disk is a flat, flexible memory device for small computer systems that closely resembles a limp 45 RPM phonograph record in a plastic jacket. Instead of storing music, it stores data digital-fashion on its grooveless surface.

The third method, comparison, involves a broad spectrum of possibilities. For our purposes we shall define it thus:

> *Comparison:* a general term that broadly covers any likening of one thing to another, whether to show similarities or differences.

This definition needs further explanation.

1. Comparison in a narrow sense refers to finding similarities; contrast refers to finding differences.
2. The two things being compared must have sufficient similarities to warrant the assessment. An old saying serves as guide: Don't compare apples and oranges.

3. The points to be mentioned or developed must be found in both elements. In a comparison of Jill and Jody, you should choose some other point than "Their command of foreign languages," if Jill knows three and Jody none. (Such a fact, if pertinent, might be mentioned in the conclusion.)

In a formal pattern, both comparison and contrast depend on the same requisites: some link between the two elements to be considered, and a sufficient number of characteristics the two have in common. In developing certain topics you may utilize both strategies.

For example, you might compare and contrast two football coaches, the link being their common goal of achieving wins.

You might compare and contrast the presidency of John Adams and John Quincy Adams, or the music of Johann Strauss the Elder and Johann Strauss the Younger.

You might compare and contrast the study required by two of your courses, the link being that they both *are* your courses. The points consist of the length of the assignments, their degrees of difficulty, and the value of each in your education.

From the examples of contrasts that follow, you will be able to judge what link is present and what points you might develop.

1. The limitations of grass tennis courts as opposed to clay or hard-surface courts.
2. The sound of one rock band as distinguished from another.
3. Differences between developing the sepia photographs of the nineteenth century and contemporary black and white photographs.
4. The significant differences between an authentic Tiffany lamp and a reproduction.
5. The five-year-old child as opposed to the four-year-old.
6. The differences in income tax benefits for a married couple and two single housemates.
7. The style of written English versus the style of spoken English.
8. The differences between two processes for polishing skills.
9. How a career differs from a job.
10. The differences between an American-made sports car and a foreign sports car of roughly the same capabilities.

The Two Possibilities of Comparing

Many writers in their papers seem more or less to happen into comparison, as opposed to ordering it up with clear-eyed deliberation. Perhaps they have never considered the two logical approaches that are possible.

The *block-by-block* approach assesses all the points of item A; then it moves to item B to assess its same points. The *point-by-point* evaluation selects one of the points held in common from the standpoint of both item A and item B before taking up the next point.

As a demonstration, we present an extremely simple topic that you will have no difficulty remembering: a contrast of the orange and the grapefruit. (As you know, both are citrus fruits having the same basic characteristics. Therefore it is valid to contrast them.) We'll assume that our reader is a resident of remotest Lapland, wholly unacquainted with these fruits.

The first step is to settle on the points that the two possess in common.

Well, they're a lot alike in appearance. Both are ball-shaped or globular, and both fall within the yellow band of the color spectrum.

What else? They are acid fruits, with tastes that range somewhere between sour and sweet.

All right; we need a third and final point. Why are they so popular as an item on our breakfast menu? Because of their nutritional value, their vitamin C.

A block-by-block tree and resulting paragraph look like this:

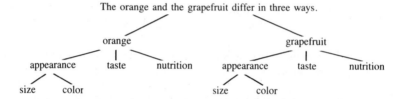

The orange and the grapefruit differ in three ways. The usual orange in appearance is about the size of a teacup in diameter and of a bright orange color. Its taste is delectably sweet and juicy. In nutrition, the orange offers a generous supply of vitamin C. The grapefruit, on the other hand, is larger in size, about the diameter of a saucer, with a pale yellow rind. Its taste is generally too sour for the average person, who likes to add sugar. Moreover, in nutrition it cannot match the vitamin C of its rival.

The preferred point-by-point tree and paragraph lay more emphasis on the contrast:

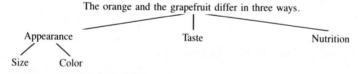

The typical orange differs from the common grapefruit in several ways. Most obviously, the fruits are dissimilar in appearance. The orange is the smaller, about teacup size, and a bright orange in color. The grapefruit, however, has the diameter of a saucer and its rind is pale yellow. Moreover, the tastes of the two fruits constitute an important difference. The orange at its best is delectably sweet and juicy; even the ripest grapefruit cannot match its flavor. For most people, the sourness of the grapefruit must be offset by sugar. As for nutrition, again the orange outstrips its chief competitor. Ounce for ounce, the orange has several times the amount of vitamin C.

(Do you find that these most obvious points suggest the Divisons of Man triad? Appearance is *physical;* taste—which hinges on personal preference—suggests *emotion;* while eating what is good for you is arguably *rational.)*

A moment's thought will convince you of the limitations of the block-by-block comparison. In *Othello* and *Hamlet,* you remember, Desdemona and Ophelia are quite similar young women, each quite important and figuring in many scenes in a five-act tragedy. A popular assignment requires a comparison of the two. It sometimes happens that a student in writing his paper will thoughtlessly choose the block-by-block approach. That means that he writes everything that can be said about Desdemona and then, leaving her entirely, launches into his material about Ophelia. By the time the reader arrives at the fact that Ophelia's father is Lord Chamberlain, a high-ranking member of the court, he has forgotten that, four pages back, he read that Desdemona's father was a senator, member of the governing council, and therefore the two courtiers are similar in rank. In effect, the student has written two separate essays.

Many times, the development of the *lower* levels of your tree (those below the main points .1, .2, .3) requires a decision about the better of the two styles. Simply for the sake of diversity, you may choose to develop the material under one main point in a block-by-block style, changing to a point-by-point style for the next main point.

Note the differences that will result from the following trees:

1.0 The brothers differ in every respect.

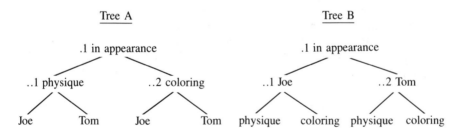

In following Tree A, you continue the point-by-point contrast. Having stated your main point .1 (They differ in appearance), you would then refer to their opposing physiques (Their physiques suggest their differences.) Not until the next lower level, that of the example, do you actually contrast the two men: Joe appears Italian (details). Tom, a Dane like our mother, is (details).

Tree B, on the other hand, indicates the lower-level block-by-block contrast. Immediately after the statement of .1, you take up the first of the two men, providing all facts available about his appearance. Then you progress to the second man, stating all details necessary about his appearance. Such treatment of appearance usually is preferable to the other, for the minor facts of coloring of hair and eyes simply do not warrant a number of extra words or sentences.

In the following programmed paragraph, you can see that the first two main points follow such a block-by-block treatment, while for variety's sake the last (and most important) point reflects Tree A.

THE BROTHERS

Our family seems to prove the unfashionable belief that ethnic stereotypes do exist. The fact that my father came from Italy and my mother from Denmark accounts for the striking differences between my two brothers.

To a stranger, they are amazingly unalike in appearance. Joe appears Italian; small, dark, voluable, given to talking with his hands. Tom, a Dane like our mother, is pale and thin, rather tall, and certainly reserved and quiet.

In their activities they are also opposed, as their hobbies and vocations indicate. Joe sings with a barbershop quartet and enjoys gourmet cooking—when he is not working with my father in the family restaurant. Tom, on the other hand, reads or studies in his spare minutes when he must leave the laboratory where he does research.

The differences in their use of time are also reflected in the conflicting values they hold. Insofar as education is concerned, Joe shrugs away the thought of college. Tom, however, is pursuing a doctorate in genetics. Toward religion they are similarly at odds: Joe, a Catholic, attends Mass once a week; Tom refuses even to discuss religion and no doubt is an atheist.

As such differences would suggest, the brothers seldom see each other, preferring to meet at our parents' house. Each one's dislike of all the other holds dear seems to be their chief similarity.

In trees that represent *comparisons,* the *minor* points generally follow the block-by-block form. That is, after stating the main points just as in a point-by-point contrast, you take up the first element of the comparison and provide its minor development in full before moving on to the other element, as in Tree B of the Joe/Tom contrast.

Earlier, when we selected our points for the orange-grapefruit contrast, you may have noticed that we could easily present a comparison of the two fruits. To find similarities usually reflects more credit on a writer than to find differences. In fact, one kind of intelligence test, the Miller Analogy Test,* requires a person to determine a wide range of similarities (which, of course, requires him also to make differences). It is no trouble at all to find two individuals different; you would gain credit for such a contrast only if there exists some strong reason for expecting similarities, as in our example of the brothers. As for the orange-grapefruit contrast, presumably our Lapp friend would be more interested in telling an orange from a grapefruit than hearing their similarities.

Note: The weakness in writing-point-by-point comparison/contrast papers lies in students' tendency to ignore the required statements of main points (.1, .2, .3), in which the two subjects being compared are linked. Casual writers often

---

*Artificial intelligence can perform many geometric analogies of the types found in such tests.

progress from the explanation level of one subject to the explanation level of the other (as in .1.1 to .2.1 and .1.2 to .2.2). Consequently, the reader feels as if he were acting as the centrally placed umpire at Wimbledon, head turning from one side to the other throughout the match. For clarity, the opponents must meet at the net at intervals—and then separate to show their similarities or differences.

In writing-point-by-point comparison papers, the beginning writer is particularly apt to sound somehow wooden and repetitive. With practice, however, he can learn to vary his expressions and his sentence structure; clarity need not exact a toll of readability.

ANALOGY

You remember that comparison/contrast generally requires the two items being evaluated to belong to the same class.

Analogy, on the other hand, may link items belonging to any two classes. Some principle underlying one serves to clarify the other. Most often, analogy makes a difficult or intangible subject comprehensible by likening it to something familiar or tangible, as we saw earlier in comparing the floppy disk with a phonograph record. Any point-by-point comparison is necessarily limited. Thus, you might compare a boomerang to the wing of a model plane, for example, but you create an analogy between a bird's wing and the plane's.

While comparison/contrast can furnish the logic of an entire paper, analogies are generally mentioned in passing, requiring only a paragraph or two. Their brevity, however, does not reflect their importance. An inspired analogy can open a window in the reader's mind to reveal lasting understanding.

Most good analogies are necessarily overused. Probably every elementary explanation of electricity has pointed out its likenesses to water. Introductory books on computers can hardly avoid the obvious comparison with the human brain. (This book, you remember, evaluates the skills of the computer programmer with the skills that you, as another kind of writer, can achieve—arguably a comparison based on an analogy.)

Analogies seldom require point-by-point development because of their brevity. Generally, the simpler, familiar element is presented first, with the more difficult following:

> Storage devices [semiconductors, ferrite cores, and so forth] are not usable unless data stored there can be retrieved when needed. In order to accomplish retrieval, each storage location has an address that identifies it just as a house address identifies a dwelling. Another comparison is a set of mailboxes in a post office. Each has a unique number which identifies the storage location. A person who wishes to store a letter in the box specifies the box number. Likewise, each set of semiconductors in a semiconductor storage or each set of cores in a core storage unit has an address. This address identifies the location so that data may be stored there, and data so stored may be retrieved. The address is a code which identifies the location for the computer circuitry.[1]

In *Taming Your Computer,* Jerome Kanter draws an analogy to make his point that not all Americans are happy to see computer systems take over the nation's industries. Some, including highly placed executives, secretly resent the inroads of the computer, opposing it in a sort of guerilla warfare:

> In the information era it behooves us to avoid the Luddite syndrome. The Luddites were an organized band of English rioters who campaigned against and destroyed laborsaving equipment in the early 1800s as a protest against lost jobs and the poor quality of work produced by the machinery. ... Today the term *Luddites* is used to refer to an individual or group who are against automation or the use of machinery to replace people or even to augment individual effort.

> ...Today's Luddites do not use physical means (though there are still intermittent instances of computer destruction) but rather more subtle methods, geared to the information era. One government worker programmed a condition in a computer program that would occur exactly sixty days after he retired. The data would trigger the execution of a program subroutine that would destroy the department's program file and central data base. In this case, a backup file system prevented this hoax from becoming a complete disaster.[2]

Analogy not only clarifies, but it can enliven and brighten technical and abstract subjects that are inherently dull. Few readers would enjoy an account of the actual mathematical steps by which, Charles L. Howe tells us, a knowledgeable criminal "misuses computers to embezzle funds, pilfer timesharing services and programs, eavesdrop on the bids of business competitors, ... print payroll checks and other documents that can be converted into ready cash," and so on. In his article "Coping with Computer Criminals," Howe (twice nominated for the Pulitzer Prize) falls back on a well-worn analogy—the nightmare—to picture the fears of those harried executives responsible for a large corporation's computer security. In surrealist scenes he weaves in some current "scams":

> His nightmare begins. He wanders through an air-conditioned data processing center, wearing a stethoscope and listening intently for a logic bomb that can erase his programs. The scene shifts. Now he roams a barren desert, vainly trying to lasso a Trojan horse trained to take a swift, vicious bite out of the corporate payroll. Sight changes to sound. Can that squeak be the opening of a trapdoor that will let outsiders in to ransack the computer for privileged passwords? A pungent aroma invades his dreams. Is it the odor of a clandestine salami technique, which is quietly taking thin slices from an assortment of corporate accounts under the computer's control? Permutation follows permutation until the alarm clock goes off.[3]

CLASSIFICATION/DIVISION

Classification is the essential process by which we bring order to a disarray of random objects. We group everything as subsets of sets, which in turn are subsets of larger sets (a mathematical concept essential to computer programming). In an office, for example, a business letter from the TXR Company is filed in a folder bearing that company's name. The folder goes in the T section of the folder allotted to correspondence from suppliers. That collection of files, in turn, is part of the current files, a chief subset of the set of all files, past and present.

As this example suggests, it is essential to classify economically for information retrieval. Imagine finding a book in a great library if the millions of books were shelved by the color of their bindings! Or just suppose students at a university were ranked according to height, as they once were in ROTC companies. What if the merchandise in a department store were arranged in alphabetical order, with hosiery at the same counter as the hose for your lawn!

Similarly, as you group the various facts that you bring together in an essay, it is necessary to settle on the most effective grouping you can devise. Why? To maximize information retrieval, as our programmer friend might say. That letter from the TXR Company that we're looking for a month hence—what if it had been tossed into a drawer marked "suppliers," along with correspondence for the past year from some twenty suppliers?

In writing a paper, the economy with which you classify constitutes one of the factors by which your reader evaluates your communication. Have you pursued your subject into its far reaches? Then, to do your search credit, you should subclassify under narrow headings.

A paper that presents the marvels of that amazing element silicon—should you classify its uses under two headings, "Industry" and "Other Uses"? No, not unless you are writing a book. You'd do well to begin with the field of electronics and narrow down from there, preferably to "Microelectronic Chips."

Let's suppose you are writing a paper on the character Athene in the *Odyssey*. For one of your main points, "Her Appearances in Human Form," you must classify some fifteen instances that you have carefully written down. What is immediately obvious is that sometimes she appears as a female, sometimes as a male. Would those be suitable subclasses?

No. They are too simple. Athene is the goddess of cunning wisdom. She assumes all these identities for special reasons. You should forget the obvious division into male and female (yes-no questions) and move into the rarer atmosphere of asking *why*. As a member of a crowd, is she simply directing people's attention to the athletic prowess of Odysseus? Does she assume the identity of the sage Mentor to voice wise advice that might properly come from him?

The slightly longer time it takes to track down such conclusions will pay off in your reader's recognition of superior classification.

Classification and division are actually two sides of the same coin. In the first, you gather together a number of different facts and group them for easier handling. In division, you take a whole—which is simply a collection of implied facts—and break it into sections for easier handling. In human reasoning processes it is difficult to distinguish between the two.

Let us say, for example, that you decide it's time you gave a party. Planning the party becomes a matter of *division:* the breaking down of the whole project into a number of different tasks. Making a list of those to be invited, planning refreshments, straightening the house, setting a date—the individual chores number at least a dozen. If you are the orderly type, you will set about *classifying* all those different things: what must be bought; what you must see to well ahead of time; what you must do the evening of the party.

As you have no doubt realized, division is a top-down process, one of the chief concerns of the program plan. Whenever you supply a cover sentence with a proof phrase, you prepare to divide your topic. To repeat: *The facts that contribute to the generality of that cover sentence must have been collected and classified beforehand—on paper.*

How, then, do we obtain facts for classification and subsequent division?

You collect them in three ways: by brainstorming yourself, by reading up on your subject, or by interviewing other people. Because the two last-named involve fact-gathering of considerable extent and effort, we shall have more to say on those subjects when we address the full-length paper. Here, however, we shall simply enlarge the suggestions we made in the last chapter.

The requirements for brainstorming yourself are quite simple. Like the necessities for good study, you must have a quiet location and a clear mind. You prepare to give yourself up to your subject. (Presumably you've been mulling it over from time to time previously.) Like Blake (in the following section), you decide to jot down absolutely everything that comes in your mind. Don't stop to judge or evaluate it; simply *write*. You can never tell when something ridiculous will spark a train of thought that arrives at a worthwhile point.

When you've "accessed" everything from storage, you begin to consider what you've written. Then you cut apart your list into strips and sort them into groups (as you'd do with file cards). The headings you provide for those groupings become your main points, the elements of your proof phrase.

REAL-LIFE WRITING: BLAKE AND THE HOME COMPUTER

Blake Robinson's family is debating the purchase of a home computer. Two members of the family argue that it would be well worth the money; one claims that it is just an expensive toy that will lie idle once the novelty wears off, and the fourth doesn't care, one way or the other.

Finally, everyone agrees to compile a list of all possible uses a home computer might serve, and then to judge whether such uses will outweigh its cost.

Blake posts a long sheet of paper on the kitchen bulletin board, headed *Benefits from a Home Computer*. He ties a pencil close by. By the time of the official family meeting a week later, the list extends all the way down the sheet.

Wordlessly, Blake proffers the list to the parent who opposes the purchase. Glancing down the many items, that person takes the pencil and draws a great X through the first ten items (in Blake's handwriting), summing up to one side: playing games.

Even so, the list includes almost a dozen strong items, as follows:

operate heating,	design programs
air-conditioning	teach vocabulary
tutor Spanish	build a robot
draw designs	keep family medical records
figure family finances	guard house
play games	figure recipes

Everybody reads it without comment.

Finally, Blake's older sister Jean looks across at Blake. "What's this thing about figuring recipes?"

"That means that if we have all the relatives for dinner on Thanksgiving, the computer will re-figure the amounts of the ingredients . . . You know, like pie for twenty-two people instead of four."

His parents exchange glances.

Finally, the parent who had opposed the computer gives in. "All right; I'll vote yes—if Blake classifies this list and writes us an informal proposal. Once he has the computer, he'll spend even less time on his writing."

"Oh, no," Blake says earnestly. "When we move on to a bigger home computer, I can practice writing right on the computer's screen!"

Blake begins immediately to plan his proposal.

First, he cuts the list into strips, one item to a strip. These he sorts into groups. "Teach vocabulary" and "tutor Spanish" share a common purpose, he sees; they go into a pile by themselves. "Guard house" and "operate heating, air-conditioning" are linked by the thought of the whole house, while figuring family finances and the recipes plus keeping family records suggests running the house.

That leaves the other four items as fun stuff—pretty heavy, compared to the other groups. Can he transfer one of them somewhere else? Well, designing programs is math, and Jean needs to work on math. He sees an even better interpretation: designing programs is really *writing* programs, isn't it? Amended, the slip now reading "writing programs" goes into the educational pile.

Now he finds himself with four groups for eleven items—a bit weak. He needs some subordination to give weight to one of his groups. Can he combine two under one heading? What about those that concern the home? The phrase "home management" comes to him. Yes, that will weight his first point nicely.

Guided by the piles of strips, Blake draws a tree and settles down to write his proposal.

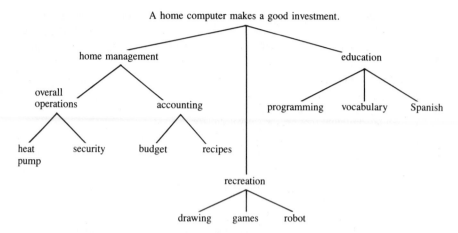

A home computer makes a good investment.

home management
   overall operations
     heat pump
     security
   accounting
     budget
     recipes

recreation
   drawing
   games
   robot

education
   programming
   vocabulary
   Spanish

In our next chapter, we'll add another major shortcut to your writing devices, a second template. The *what it is* template is a masterly guide to clarifying what you know and want to write, adaptable to a wide variety of situations.

First, however, we'll finish discussing the remaining kinds of development that will contribute to the new template's supports: definition, cause/effect, process.

SUMMARY

Writing is primarily a matter of making decisions or selections. Computers perform a somewhat similar process in response to the programmer's *IF/THEN— ELSE* command. They compare, select, classify, and set up cause/result situations, suggesting the importance of these techniques in exploring and developing thought on paper.

In comparing/contrasting a pair of subjects, two approaches are possible: (a) The writer presents the points of one in its entirety; then he takes up the same points that are found in the other. (b) The writer refers to one point at a time in terms of both subjects, before going on to the next point.

Analogy is a form of comparison that requires only a limited comparison, but it should be striking and original.

Classification and division are two sides to the same coin. Classification requires random objects (or facts) to be linked according to their similarities under a heading. Division requires a "whole" to be separated into parts according to their differences.

ASSIGNMENTS

1. Draw structure trees for the following contrasts. (You may ignore the last sentence in each case, which constitutes a conclusion.)

A. With one exception, attending college as an adult woman proves to be a less difficult venture than that experienced by most younger coeds. Most notably, the experiences differ in the degree of commitment a student exhibits toward her chosen field of study. Simply having lived longer and experienced more of life, an older woman is better able to judge the area of academia for which she is best suited. Girls right out of high school, on the other hand, are often buffeted by parental and societal forces that sometimes propel them into careers of someone else's choosing. Older and younger students also vary in their seriousness of purpose. Because the adult woman possesses a more secure sense of direction, she will have assignments ready on time and will usually top the curve on quizzes and examinations. Coeds in late adolescence must deal with all the identity-forming tasks of that period and thus are continually worried about who shall take them to the ball game on Saturday, who might be in the next room in the library, and what personality they must display on any given day. Time demands are not as great for the younger student, however, and in that respect she has an advantage over her older counterpart. Adult women typically have family and household responsibilities that make it difficult to budget time for study and for library research. Younger students, in contrast, are generally free from family and housekeeping chores, giving them more flexibility with time demands. Still, harried schedules notwithstanding, the older woman student, because of her maturity and more refined sense of herself, experiences a more rewarding and less difficult academic career than does a younger student.

B. Continuing Education courses differ appreciably from credit courses in several ways. Such non-credit courses make no real demands on their students like the long assignments and regular attendance typical of credit courses. Nor do they exert pressure in class. The atmosphere is more like a club meeting where everyone is relaxed and vocal. Moreover, they involve little expense. A Continuing Ed course that meets two hours a week for fifteen weeks costs only $75, and no text or extra fee is involved. Credit courses, on the other hand, demand regular attendance and lengthy assignments. The student who ignores either one may find himself failing the course. Another factor involved is a certain amount of in-class stress where discussion is invited. Students feverishly take notes, avoiding the professor's eye, fearing he will call on them and thus come to realize their meagre knowledge of the material. Most obvious is the cost factor, the credit courses being far more expensive. Courses counting toward a degree in a sixteen-week semester are estimated at $200 an hour, $600 a course, to which is added the additional expense of books and perhaps a fee. Continuing Ed courses are like dress rehearsals for the real scene.

2. The tree for "The Brothers" paper is more extended than any you have encountered thus far. Study the third and fourth divisions as they are reproduced below, noting the organization of the lower levels of the two points. How are those divisions implied or stated?

Following the exact sentence patterns (even the same words for the points, if you wish), substitute facts about two people you know who, though closely related, reveal the same sort of differences as Joe and Tom.

> In their activities they are also opposed, as their hobbies and vocations indicate. Joe sings with a barbershop quartet and enjoys gourmet cooking—when he is not working with my father in the family restaurant. Tom, on the other hand, reads or studies in his spare minutes when he must leave the laboratory where he does research.

The differences in their use of time are also reflected in the conflicting values they hold. Insofar as education is concerned, Joe shrugs away the thought of college. Tom, however, is pursuing a doctorate in genetics. Toward religion they are similarly at odds: Joe, a Catholic, attends Mass once a week; Tom refuses even to discuss religion and no doubt is an atheist.

3. Devise a tree and write a paragraph comparing or contrasting two items. You may choose your own subjects or write on one of the following:

    (a) a course you had in high school and the same course in college

    (b) the teaching methods of two of your professors

    (c) dating and being engaged

    (d) watching some sport on television and attending a game or match

    (e) living in the city and living in the suburbs

4. Give thought to two different things in which you perceive a similarity that others might miss (like a chess game and a sonata). Write a paragraph of analogy that points out the likeness, beginning with the sentence _____ _____ is like _____ _____. Try to be as original as possible.

5. Classify the following reasons for which Americans attend professional conventions. Give your divisions suitable headings and then draw a tree that would generate a paper.

cement good will for company	make personal contacts that could advance personal career
mix with people who share the same interests	learn new methods of solving professional problems
avoid penalties of being absent	get expense-free vacations
like to "party"	pick brains of competitors
escape family	generate business not available in other ways

NOTES

1. Gordon B. Davis, *Introduction to Computers* (New York: McGraw Hill, 1977), p. 195.

2. Jerome Kanter, *Taming Your Computer* (Englewood Cliffs, N.J.: Prentice-Hall, 1981), pp. 226-227.

3. Charles L. Howe, "Coping with Computer Criminals," *Datamation*, 28, no. 1. (January 1982), 119.

4

USING ANOTHER SPECIAL PATTERN

GOAL: to acquire additional methods of development and to apply them in the What-it-is template

We have been investigating the thought processes that are duplicated in written communication, you remember. In this chapter we shall touch on three more: definition, cause/result, and process. By then you will understand the various kinds of development that you may summon as supports for the important What-it-is template that awaits you, later in this chapter.

You will find this new template remarkably helpful, both in academic assignments and in managerial writing. Any time that an assignment allows you to choose your own subject, you have available the pattern for its main points, both as you seek material and in the actual writing process. Even for papers on restricted topics it is almost always adaptable. In your professional career as well, the What-it-is pattern guides you into the essential factors of a new product or method under consideration.

First, let us consider those methods of development we mentioned.

DEFINITION

In processes resembling those with which we sought to identify the Saab (in the preceding chaper), a dictionary traditionally defines an entry by classification and differentiation. That is, it informs the reader of the entry's general grouping; then it divides this item from other members of its class by explaining its differences from other members of that class. A dictionary provides other information as well: the word's part of speech, some of its synonyms, its etymology (origin and history), and, where necessary, its debated uses. (You might look up *presently,* for example.)

As you may find definition necessary in your writing, most often it figures as a fairly limited section of a report or article. Its purpose is to explain a word or term that otherwise might not be clear to the reader. Within limits, a writer may choose to invent a term, as Horace Walpole invented *serendipity,* or limit it to some special meaning, thus:

> The reference to "fox hunters," in Mercredi's intention, evokes an image far different from that pictured on TV, where red- or black-coated socialites on sleek horses stream across a picturesque countryside. Instead, his fox hunters meet at night on some mountain-top, where they sit comfortably drinking around a fire, listening to the rise and fall of their individual hounds' baying off in the distance.

In an example that may surprise you, early writers in the women's liberation movement, needing a word for male traditionalists, simply appropriated the word *chauvinist.* As dictionaries defined the word in 1969, for example, this assigned meaning ignores the etymology (origin and history) of the word:

> *chauvinism:* military and boastful devotion to and glorification of one's country; fanatical patriotism. [French, *chauvinisme,* after Nicolas *Chauvin,* legendary French solider extremely devoted to Napoleon.]
>
> *American Heritage Dictionary*

Because dictionaries must reflect usage, however, contemporary dictionaries obediently report the word's current application.

You may find it necessary to explain a technical term to readers not familiar with professional jargon. Thus, a dictionary of computer terms intended for the layman provides this definition:

> *light pen:* a photosensitive device that can cause the computer to change or modify the display on a cathode-ray tube display device. As the display information is selected by the operator, the light pen signals the computer, using a pulse. The computer then instructs other points or lines to be plotted on the screen following the pen movements.[1]

In explaining the device to a young teen-ager, a writer might simplify even further:

> *light pen:* a slender flashlight device that shines a narrow beam of light at a computer screen. A light pen can feed in new data, change and move lines and curves, answer questions, etc.

Any definition you provide of a term important to your paper should of course appear early in the paper, rather than as a sort of postscript to its use.

CAUSE/RESULT

So far as writing is concerned, cause/result, problem/solution, and stimulus/response present no problems of organization. Each simply asks and answers a question:

Cause/Result   Why? Why does a plane fall when it encounters a wind sheer?

Problem/Solution   How? How can data security be achieved?

Stimulus/
Response   What? What happens if you put frog legs into a hot pan?

Where you present a single cause (or result) and several results (or causes), your situation matches the program plan pattern:

In the following examples, parentheses indicate causes; brackets, results.

1. [Genetic mutation] is achieved by a (three-step process).
2. The Helvetians' (lack of resources) limited their [retaliation] to three minor skirmishes.
3. The [success of Ultra] resulted from the (special qualities) of its Chiefs and Indians.
4. The [bridge disaster] might have been avoided (had the contractor observed three precautions).
5. Because (Halley's comet) was thought to portend disaster, people reacted with [several kinds of violence].

A more difficult situation arises when each of several causes produces one or more results:

In the three battles, each leader suffered a noteworthy loss.

A similar tree accounts for such an article as this, in which a result becomes a cause:

THE KIND OF BOOK I LIKE BEST—GOTHIC NOVELS

Why do I like gothic novels? Because they provide thrills, mystery, and eventual happiness for their heroine—a heroine who reacts to horror with my fears, to dire secrets with my need to know, and to romance with all women's longing to be loved.

When masked threats and evil omens shroud the gloomy mansion to which this nice girl has been lured, my fight-or-flee system flashes red alert. My heart pounds; goosebumps tighten my chilled skin; I race over the pages, aware of more ghastly horrors yet to come.

When she hears of mysterious bloody murder that involves money, she pokes around and looks for clues, with curiosity I recognize. I, too, would ask the thoughtless tip-off question, snoop in forbidden places, venture to some dangerous rendezvous.

Then, when she finds she has misjudged that strong, reserved, attractive man who rescues her and finally speaks of love, my heart glows, too, in neon lights. I contemplate the pulsing joys ahead for her, with this masterful, rich husband. I smile at the thought of their future children in their happy home.

Why do I like Gothic novels? Just because ... For a few hours, they hold a mirror to my strongest drives, my basic hopes and fears, my need to know. And so I—and millions like me—continue to read and make Gothic writers rich!

TIME AND SPACE

Development of a paper by time is closely linked to process and to simple narrative; they all say, "This happened, and then this, and then that—" Similarly, development by space is often a matter of description. While time and space are termed "natural" means of development, the use of organization and some thoughtful variation serves to enhance their simplicity.

The most essential requirement of any of these is to make sure the reader knows where he is in any given time-period or space. The untrained writer, his mind full of the events that took place at a particular time, tends not to mention that important factor until after he has poured forth his facts. By that time, the reader's mind has already classified—or attempted to classify—those facts with the previous time period. Therefore, much of the impact of those facts is wasted. Few readers will go back to reread the sentence or paragraph in light of the adjusted date.

Time and space, then, belong at the beginning of the facts you attribute to them. In a paragraph organized by time periods, this becomes merely a matter of a prepositional phrase at the beginning of a sentence.

No one knows precisely when golf was first played in Scotland. In 1457, records show that the Scottish parliament voiced stern disapproval of those who preferred it to more useful archery practice. Fourteen years later, parliament called on civil and religious authorities to "cry it down and not use it." By 1491, golf's popularity led to a decree that listed highly unpleasant "pains and penalties" for its impractical devotees.

In longer papers (other than those presenting a process), it is usually advisable to avoid main points that are time periods. If you are writing on a literary work, for example, you run a considerable risk of simply re-telling the story, an undertaking that both you and your reader come to regret. In a biography, you are likely to oppress your reader with the weight of all those years that lie ahead.

(For this reason, many applications for creative jobs or internships require an autobiographical essay, an effective test of the applicant's ability to manage the tedious march of time.)

How, then, can you handle a long biographical paper?

If your problem insists on organization in terms of blocks of time, you can shift them out of order. For most notables who would be your subject, it is likely that his life can be divided into three time periods: preparation, achievement, and diminution. Conceivably, you begin with the period of achievement and, at suitable intervals, dip into the preparation stage and the period of old age, returning to take up the achievement period again.

A better arrangement is to single out certain factors from that achievement period and then examine them in terms of time. (You can hardly do otherwise if your subject shows no sign of descending from his peak of achievement.)

Suppose, for example, our friend Court decides to write on Steven Spielberg. Because he, too, would like to be a director, he has read everything available about Spielberg's early home life and the characteristics that suggested his later success. It seems now like a good idea to relate these personal facts to the major films. First, then, he must determine the most important characteristics that the various productions have in common.

While Court has viewed the films as many times as his finances will allow, he carefully studies the major reviews and interviews. Eventually, he decides that Spielberg's power lies in his ability to depict certain qualities that are true to a typical American childhood: a warm home-life, fears that haunt even a protected child, the excitement of adventure and make-believe. Court finds that he can demonstrate these factors both in Spielburg's childhood and in the various films. But how will he move back and forth in time?

He sees that under each main point (a quality) can be two subpoints: *then* and *now.* That is, he'll establish the main point firmly, allude to its universality, its appeal to the public (perhaps in terms of the number of admissions sold, or some other proof). Then he'll drop back into Spielberg's youth and his experiences. For the other subpoint, he'll call attention to their reflection in the various films.

(He determines not to succumb to the lure of psychoanalyzing the director. It's enough to point out similarities.)

Court's structure tree looks like this:

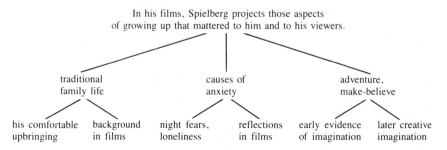

A final word on *time:* Regardless of your points, don't let the subject of your biography die early in the paper. You may deal with his mortal illness anywhere—but wait until the final point or the conclusion to let him make his final bow.

Space

Space, although a natural order, requires a basic consideration: a logical progression forward, or an orderly withdrawal. While anthropologist Dorothy Lee refers to a Papuan tribe that has no concept of a straight line, our culture finds it essential. Here is an example of the near-to-far or far-to-near principle.

Suppose we are writing an article on a national figure. In the section assigned to relationships with others, we envision him at the center of a circle. Around him orbit his concerns in widening order: his family, his friends, the public. Here, it seems logical to move from the core outward.

But suppose that, in the case of a prominent politician, his geniality is a false front. To the general public he appears warm, patient, genial, caring. To his aides and associates, however, he is relentless in his requirements, demanding unstinting time and energy, as if they had no personal commitments. To his wife and children, he can be counted on only when news-media people are on hand.

In such a situation, to start at the periphery (the public) and move inward (to his family) would be effective, for we would achieve an unvoiced contrast between the expected and the real.

A similar logical order is necessary in presenting an object or a scene for the reader to envision.

Let us suppose that you notice an extremely attractive member of the opposite sex at some distance from you. You perceive overall appearance first— general build, height, stance. Then, as the person approaches, you see lesser details—coloring and features. Finally, you note less obvious indications of personality. Desirably, you would follow the same order in describing the individual on paper.

A typical assignment in freshman composition calls for students to write a paragraph of description about their dorm room. When you consider the typical small room overflowing with the belongings of two persons of different tastes, this is no easy assignment.

Should the student station himself and his reader in the corridor doorway and then progress around the room, mentioning everything he passes?

No. Such an assignment needs logical handling. In this case, a time oganization works well.

That is, the student should first present the bare room as it was originally constructed—size, windows, doors. Next, he places the school's furniture in the room—beds, chests, desks. Finally, he can add personal belongings the roommates brought with them. In this way, the reader is oriented before he is distracted by the sheer number of items crowded into the room.

In writing, space can often be dealt with in terms of time, because of their close relationship:

Halfway through the book, Tess's life begins a downward slide into misery and death.

A final word: Remember to furnish the necessary information about those basic coordinates of time and place *before* you provide the information that pertains to them. While fairy- and folk tales are said to be the composition of an illiterate society, keep in mind their traditional beginning: Once upon a time, in a kingdom far away—

PROCESS

A process is by definition a series of actions, changes, or functions that bring about an end or result.

From the standpoint of writing, there are two basic kinds of process that you may need to write. The first is descriptive in purpose. While it requires accuracy, it is not intended to direct the reader to whatever end-result the process accomplishes.

Thus, a writer for *Science* might carefully allude to the many processes by which a crystal of pure silicon becomes an electronics device. For all his accuracy, his laymen readers are not enabled to achieve the same result.

Similarly, we read descriptions of the steps by which a computer plays backgammon with human opponents. Yet we cannot follow such steps as these to program our home computer:

> The computer moves are determined by sections of priority move searches. The computer tries [in this order] to move two men together to form a blocked point, to hit the other player (you), to move safely to a previously blocked point, or to move the farthest man. ... It can accept or refuse a double, or suggest a double to you.[2]

The other kind of process, of course, is that which enables us to achieve a desired result. It stipulates with detail and clarity the steps that must be followed. Examples of this kind of process are abundant: the directions that enable us to build a bookcase or to mix a cake, to assemble some gadget that comes to us in bits and pieces, to do the shag, or to achieve self-hypnosis.

Here (translated from the computer language Fortran) is the process, the algorithm, that a computer follows in playing a perfect game of ticktacktoe:

Algorithm A (The computer plays X.)

A.1. Perform the first applicable step which follows.

A.2. Search for two X's in a row. If found, then make three X's in a row.

A.3. Search for two O's in a row. If found, then block them with an X.

A.4. Search for two rows that intersect with an empty square, each of which contains one X and no O's. If found, then place an X on the intersection.

A.5. Search for two rows that intersect at an empty square, each of which contains one O and no X's. If found, then place an X on the intersection.

A.6. Search for a vacant corner square. If found, then place an X on the vacancy.
A.7. Search for a vacant square. If found, then place an X on the vacancy.[3]

In the natural order of things, process is unbroken. Your reader, however, will understand and appreciate your communication considerably more if you divide this progression into stages. Professional writers regularly treat a list of directions as sections and paragraphs. You may follow their example to your advantage.

Consider the simple steps for building a bookcase or baking a cake. What stages have they in common? There is the *preparation:* For the bookcase, the lumber must be selected and sawed, nails, sandpaper, stain, etc., purchased, the necessary tools laid out. For the cake, assembling and measuring ingredients, preheating the oven, greasing the pans.

Then follows the *assembly:* The frame of the bookcase is fitted together, the shelves properly mortised or supported. The ingredients of the cake are blended in several steps.

Finally, there is the *finishing.* The bookcase is sanded, the nailheads depressed and cavities filled; it is stained and varnished in a series of applications. The cake is baked at a certain temperature for a certain length of time. It is cooled in its pan or on a rack; the icing is made and applied.

(If you question the need for breaking up six or seven steps into such obvious groups as these, you have only to consider the relative ease with which you learn the ten digits of a telephone number [including the area code] as opposed to memorizing ten unbroken numbers.)

Abstract processes are similarly divided. The intellectual activity of a chess game is discussed as if it were presented in three divisions: the opening strategy, the middle period that seeks to justify that strategy, and the end of the game. A sonata moves through exposition, development, and recapitulation, thus breaking up its "message."

At this point, you have met the techniques that are most important in developing and exploring thought.

You are ready to make the acquaintance of our second template.

THE WHAT-IT-IS PATTERN

In a small child's questions, in school classes, in ordinary advertising as well as highly esteemed essays, you have met the three divisions of this new template, although not in combination:

> *What it is*
> *What it does (or achieves)*
> *Why it's needed*

While the Divisions of Man triad served to analyze a given person or personification, this new template deepens and extends potential subject matter to include subjects that are inanimate: institutions, organizations, systems, objects newly experienced.

Moreover, the two templates together may be combined in a grid that extends their assistance beyond that of either template alone. That is, they structure such knowledge as you already possess; then they go on to suggest additional avenues that may prove profitable to pursue.

First, however, suppose we view this triad and its applications singly, for as a device it is highly useful. Conceivably, it could serve all your writing needs while you're in college.

Its Widespread Use

As you watch TV commercials, as you read articles in your favorite popular magazine, as you research information in books or reference works, you encounter information organized in terms of *being, doing,* and *knowing,* three of the most basic states associated with human beings.

The first two are fundamental to any given culture, for they are rooted deep within its language system. Some linguists classify a given language and the thought processes it represents as oriented toward one of those essential states: *being* (stasis) or *doing* (action). In turn, this basic factor markedly affects the given society, which perceives and structures its world and the patterning of its relationships in terms of one or the other.

Americans, for example, tend to name and define according to *function* (doing). By contrast, anthropologist Dorothy Lee shows us that the Wintu Indians of California name and define according to the *appearance* (being) of a given thing. Thus, an overturned basket, a thatched hut, and an automobile share the same stem *muk* because in profile they share the same sort of curve.[4]

Knowing is perception by the senses or the mind, so that in some sense it is the culmination of being and doing. The great French thinker Descartes asked the essential question, "Can we know?" and answered it, "I think [doing], therefore I am [being]."

If you question the effectiveness of our template, you have only to watch TV ads, where the success of a communication pattern can be validated in purchase-power.

What it is:	Here it is at last—the new *Caliph Coffee!*
What it does:	*Caliph* gives you full-bodied flavor
Why it's needed:	yet never keeps you awake with jittery coffee nerves!

An ad in your favorite magazine makes this point:

What it is:	Refinements in the new Pontiac's body design
What it does:	have been engineered
Why it's needed:	to give you improved fuel economy!

As you pick up the new issue of *Psychology Today,* you read the blurb on the cover:

Subliminal Stimulation—What it is, what it does, and why it's banned on TV.

If you were to analyze the feature stories in your newspaper, you would find that a certain number follow the What-it-is structure, as these do:

Cover Statement: Wallyball provides a new challenge to handball aficionados.
What it is: Combination of volleyball and handball
What it does: Offers fast action, diversity
Why it's needed: Provides a new and difficult challenge

Cover Sentence: Soon you'll be able to mix up a quart of custardy-rich ice cream mix at considerable savings.
What it is: A new process for making ice cream mix developed by a university scientist
What it does: Ends the present requirement for refrigeration during transit and shelf-life
Why it's needed: Refrigeration is expensive and a waste of energy.

Cover Sentence: In a given factory, automation by a transfer machine can replace five hundred workers.
What it is: A series of 500 work stations, extending the length of a football field
What it does: Assembles the product with speed and accuracy
Why it's needed Takes over what humans consider deadly routine; ends various personnel problems

The what-it-is template will serve for almost any sort of report that provides information with which the reader is unfamiliar, as in an encyclopedia's explanation of the boomerang:

What it is: The boomerang is a weapon of carved wood, generally associated with the Australian aborigines and named for a tribe in New South Wales. Similar throwing sticks were known to the ancient Egyptians and to some African tribes. Two types are found: the war or non-returning boomerang and the hunting boomerang, which does return.

In shape, the latter resembles a lazy L, the angle between the arms being about 105°. In size, the returning weapon measures about two feet from tip to tip; the war device about three feet.

What it does: The successful flight of the weapon depends largely on its skew and on the carefully crafted arms, which are contoured like the wings of a plane. The thrower hurls it overhanded, providing with a snap of the wrist a special spin that imparts lift and stability.

After being thrown, the hunting boomerang travels straight for thirty yards or so, spinning vertically. Then it describes a great circle of some fifty yards in its return to the thrower.

Why it's needed: In the aborigines' continuing struggle for food, the boomerang offered a second chance at the prey if the first throw missed. Against an enemy, the larger missile had ample force to kill, even at a considerable distance.

Safeguards and Variations

As you read the foregoing examples, you probably noticed how their individual development would draw on those patterns that you learned earlier—definition, comparison/contrast, analogy, cause/result, process. In your own writing, you will choose among them for whatever your material seems to require.

Suppose we look at some safeguards that you will need to consider, along with some useful variations.

SETTING CAREFUL BOUNDARIES. As you plan your paper, you'll be wise to set boundaries between the three sections of the template. Otherwise, you're likely to find yourself explaining what a thing *does* when you think that you're still on the what-it-is stage, or implying why it's needed when you describe what it does. Such boundaries require thought on your part, for in many cases, simply to mention what a thing is necessarily refers to its activity. (Again, our robust American emphasis on *doing!*) A karate teacher is one who teaches karate; a coding machine is a mechanism that reduces language to gibberish; a ranger ranges, and so on.

In fact, when you turn to an early chapter in a book on programming your home computer, you find its first heading to be *what it is,* and immediately under that you read:

> In simplest terms, a computer is a device that receives information, manipulates it, and sends it back out. If it doesn't do all three of these operations, it just isn't a computer.[5]

Since a hand-operated eggbeater is also a "device," the writer clearly intends the definition to be a matter of the actions this particular device performs.

VARIATIONS. Here is a tip to handle that sort of problem. If your explanation of the first section shades into action, then you are at liberty to change the interpretation of the second section. What it *does* can become What it *achieves,* as suggested in the following digests of newspaper stories:

Cover Sentence:	A proposed gun control measure offers the most radical solution yet to the problem of the Saturday Night Special.
What it is:	Suggested limitations on the manufacture of this type of gun
What it achieves:	Eventual unavailability of such guns to the public
Why it's needed:	Latest statistics of violent deaths; inadequacy of laws

In the situation where you use *achieves,* you may want to change the order of the sections, delaying the achievements until the last point, for a good ending.

Cover Sentence:	American students receive far less training in mathematics and science than do Russian students.

What it is:	Present requirements of math and sci-
(What the requirements are)	ence in each country.
What it achieves	Implied cause/result: inferior training
(What the requirements [don't] achieve)	for American youth in contrast to Russian
Why it is needed:	Contrasted careers and later productiv-
(Why better requirements are needed)	ity show Americans in bad light

Other slight changes will suggest themselves from time to time. You may change the order of the three sections; often it works well to show *need* before you show present achievement. There is no reason to be rigid with your interpretation; in the book on programming we cited earlier, the second section (following *What It Is)* is headed *How It Works,* which often makes a good second point. Be sure to check your wording carefully, in order to avoid making two points say virtually the same thing.

THE UNCHANGING IDENTITY OF *IT.* Take care that, in all three sections of your template, you imply the same antecedent for the pronoun *it.* That antecedent can be masculine, feminine, or neuter; it can be singular or plural,but in all three divisions it should be consistent.

Moreover, the *it* of the triad must always represent the real subject of the paragraph (or section). That subject is sometimes the object of the verb, as in the second of the two following sentences, where the discussion covers the duties of such an employee:

1. The post of victim's advocate should be created by the city.   (subject)
2. The city should create the post of victim's advocate.   (object)

THE NEED TO LIMIT YOUR IMPLICATIONS. If you write easily, you may find yourself packing facts into your key sentences to the extent that they promise more than you intend to deliver. Note the number of possibilities for discussion that similar cover sentences for a template paper may suggest:

1. Many psychologists believe in human imprinting.
2. Many psychologists believe imprinting to be responsible for certain behavior patterns.
3. Many psychologists believe that the imprinting of basic behavior patterns takes place in certain critical periods of growth.

In 1, you suggest that human imprinting will be your subject— what it is, what it achieves, why it takes place. "Many psychologists" is simply a convenient generalization; you need not name names.

In 2, you seem to suggest the reader's pre-existing understanding of imprinting; it is the behavior patterns that receive emphasis. Because the statement is highly debatable on the professional level, you seem also committed to identifying those professionals you mention.

In 3, you commit yourself to so many obligations that to write a template paper would be almost impossible. It would be very difficult indeed to keep your boundaries straight. Key sentences are like promissory notes; you obligate yourself to deliver certain things, so watch your wording.

REAL-LIFE WRITING

When Patsy Pepperell was a tree-climbing tomboy of eight, she witnessed the brutal killing of a neighbor, a gentle old lady of whom Patsy was very fond. Although Patsy was carefully questioned during the subsequent investigation, she was never able to provide any meaningful identification of the murderer, although it was obvious that she had seen him clearly.

Now that she is fifteen, she has begun to have terrible dreams in which she sees the crime re-enacted. Usually, she is in the oak tree, as she was then, frozen with horror. Just as the killer turns to leave, so that she must see his face, she wakens, trembling and crying.

To end such trauma, her psychiatrist considers it essential to hypnotize Patsy. In such therapy, she can be induced to re-enact the entire experience and thereby rob it of its continuing threat.

While her mother has agreed to the treatment, her father—living in another city—is opposed. He fears that, once hypnotized, Patsy's mind will be weakened, leaving her more susceptible to dominance by undesirable acquaintances. The psychiatrist, Dr. Young, has agreed to write him, explaining what therapeutic hypnotism is, what it does to the patient's mind, and why it's needed in Patsy's case.

Here is a portion of the letter he writes:

> Therapeutic hypnotism can best be explained as an induced state in which the objective or governing aspect of the patient's mind is induced to retire in favor of the subjective aspect. In Patsy's case, such treatment will enable her to recall a disturbing experience that can then be dealt with on a conscious level.
>
> By this definition, it is necessary to conceive of the mind as having two differing aspects, the dominant objective and the submissive subjective. Ordinarily, the objective makes decisions, for, along with its control of the senses, it can reason both inductively and deductively. By contrast, the subjective aspect is retiring; it accepts the generalizations supplied by the objective, for its reasoning is always deductive. The subjective does, however, control two important aspects of thought—memory and dreaming.
>
> To achieve the hypnotic state, the two aspects must shift places, as they normally do in sleep. By means of the doctor's suggestions, which induce a sleep-like situation, the objective is lulled into quiescence, leaving in command the subjective—with its control of memory. Conditioned to accept generalizations, the subjective accepts the doctor's careful directions (in this case) to regress through levels of time. Finally, it reaches the scene of the traumatic memory, blocked off protectively by the objective. Once laid bare, like the source of an infection, the memory can be treated and, eventually, eased to bearable proportions.

In Patsy's situation, this sort of memory retrieval is desperately needed. Although she shows signs of remembering on her own, therapeutic hypnosis affords a means of cutting short her suffering and dread. Under professional care, her trauma of remembering can be mitigated; otherwise, she must face it alone.

I urge you to consider this memory as some cancer that must not go untreated . . .[6]

The What-it-is template opens a wide vista of subjects to which it can be applied. You will find it remarkably effective in shortening and directing your research for a library paper, as we shall point out later.

In our next chapter, you will see how smoothly the program plan paragraph expands into a full-length paper. Simple formulas for introductions and conclusions serve to launch such a paper effectively and conclude it favorably.

SUMMARY

In addition to comparison/contrast, analogy, classification and division, the traditional methods of development include definition of terms unfamiliar to your reader, cause/result, natural time, space, and process (of which there are two kinds: descriptive and directive). Desirably, on-going space or time should be sectioned by the writer to avoid monotony. Because the reader must be able to associate what he reads with the proper time or space element, it is important to provide that information in advance of the material to which it applies.

The What-it-is template lends itself to a wide variety of uses. Almost any subject can be developed in terms of what it is, what it does (or achieves), and why (or how) it's needed. For good results, the writer should delimit the sections to avoid confusion, either on his part or that of the reader. In the interest of clarity, the pronoun *it* in each case should refer to the same noun, the subject of the paper, or something pertaining to it.

Because key sentences represent the writer's obligations to his reader, they work best if worded simply.

ASSIGNMENTS

1. In a good encyclopedia, look up several of the following and then write an extended definition on any three that interest you:

cybernetics	mandrake	farthingale
cochineal	Valkyrie	the Fibonacci sequence
tsunami	lemming	

2. As process, write a paragraph that would enable the reader to lace a shoe if he had never previously seen it done.

3. In a short paper that provides three separate causes and corresponding results, answer one of the following:

  a. Why people laugh at clowns
  b. Why Americans glorify the Old West
  c. Why exotic animals (wolves, lions, ocelots, etc.) should not be kept as pets
  d. What makes a good talk-show host
  e. Why people are collectors
  f. Why social promotion should (or should not) be ended

4. The following article from the *Encyclopedia of Computer Science* follows a design such as we have recently discussed. Develop its structure tree in terms of the particular development.

GAMES ON COMPUTERS[7]

When the earliest digital computers were built, scientists immediately became fascinated with the possibility of having them play such games as chess, checkers, and ticktacktoe. Although this sort of activity proved to be a great deal of fun, the scientists were not just playing around; as it turns out, there are several good reasons to study game playing by computers.

The first reason relates to the popular conception of computers as "giant brains." Even the earliest digital computers could do arithmetic and make decisions at a rate thousands of times faster than humans could. Thus, it was felt that computers could be set up to perform intelligent activities such as to translate French to English, recognize sloppy handwriting, and play chess. At the same time, it was realized that if computers could not perform these tasks, then they could not be considered intelligent by human standards. A new scientific discipline arose from these considerations and became known as "artificial intelligence."

A second reason involves man's understanding of his own intelligence. It is conjectured that computer mechanisms for game playing will bear a resemblance to human thought processes. If this is true, then game-playing computers can help us understand how human minds work.

Another reason for studying games is that they are well-defined activities. Most games use very simple equipment and have a simple set of rules that must be followed. Usually, the ultimate goal (winning) can be very simply defined. Thus, a computer can be easily set up to know the rules of any board game or card game. This allows the computer scientist to devote more effort to the problem of getting the computer to play an intelligent game.

There is also a practical payoff from computer game-playing studies. Specific techniques developed in programming a computer to play games have been applied to other more practical problems. To cite a few, methods of search, which are used to consider alternative moves in chess, have been adapted to find the correct path through a switching network or the correct sequence of steps for an assembly line. Learning methods developed for a checker playing program have been used to recognize elementary parts of spoken speech. It is felt that the mechanisms of intelligence are general purpose, and therefore the borrowing of techniques from one application to another will continue in the field of artificial intelligence.

NOTES

1. Michael Hordeski, *Illustrated Dictionary of Microcomputer Terminology* (Blue Ridge Summit, Pa.: Tab Books, 1978), p. 149.

2. Paul Friedman, *Computer Programs in Basic* (Englewood Cliffs, N.J.: Prentice-Hall, Inc., 1981),p. 36.

3. Anthony Ralston, ed., *Encyclopedia of Computer Science* (New York: Petrocelli/ Charter, 1976), p. 584.

4. Dorothy Lee, *Freedom and Culture* (Englewood Cliffs, N.J.: Prentice-Hall, 1959), p. 108.

5. Paul Bryan, *Programming Your Computer* (Blue Ridge Summit, Pa.: Tab Books, 1982), p. 75.

6. Raphael H. Rhodes, *Hypnosis: Theory, Practice, and Application* (Secaucus, N.J.: Citadel Press, 1950), pp. 16, 22. The author's explanation of hypnosis is not necessarily that of other psychologists. It is endorsed, however, by Dr. Foster Kennedy, Professor of Neurology, Cornell University College of Medicine, and the Director of the Neurological Service at Bellevue Hospital, New York.

7. Ralston, p. 583.

5
COMBINING PARAGRAPHS FOR THE FULL-LENGTH PAPER

GOAL: To write a full-length paper, including introduction and conclusion

At this stage, you have acquired the skills that enable you to write a full-length paper—introductory paragraph, several body paragraphs, and conclusion.

Such a paper is simply an expansion of the pattern you have learned for the paragraph. Instead of one paragraph, you structure and write five. Even the introduction and conclusion represent modifications of that pattern.

The general-to-specific development of relationships does not change; in a long paper, each element simply carries more responsibility.

The result is a unified, coherent essay possessing clear internal organization—a highly desirable characteristic all too often missing from student compositions.

To demonstrate an agreeable transition from paragraph to full-length paper, then, becomes our concern in this chaper. In addition, we shall examine various types of introductions and conclusions.

THE TRANSITION: THE FULL-LENGTH PAPER

Any number of analogies exist that manifest the relationship between the program plan paragraph and the full-length paper. The most apt, perhaps, is to consider the paragraph a scale model for the paper. As we said earlier, the paragraph is an essay in miniature; except for coverage area, the two are structured alike:

Both have an initial cover sentence that controls the paper's development.

Both have a limited set of main points that section the material.

Both explain each main point individually, and (usually) both provide examples.

Their differences are simply a matter of size or responsibility. It is as if the governor of a state had become president, so that the departments over which he presides have moved from the state level to the federal, an expansion of authority.

The cover sentence now controls a paper of several pages from its paragraph of introduction.

Each main point is supported, not by one or two sentences, but by at least a paragraph.

Each explanation and its examples fill out a paragraph.

To cite a very simple analogy, it's as if you set out to make Brunswick stew for twenty people instead of the usual four. While you increase the ingredients considerably, the proportions—the relationship of each to each—remain the same.

As you accomplish this expansion, however, you need to keep in mind a simple precaution: You must stress relationships more in the full-length paper than in the shorter version, simply because your lines of communication are stretched farther apart. You will need to make transitions obvious between your points—and within the paragraphs—to remind your reader of your progress.

The Computer Analogy

In our continuing comparison of the programmer and the beginning writer, it is interesting to note that the novice programmer follows this same sort of expansion.

Like you, he practices miniature programs that contain the basic, essential logic that he will subsequently employ. When he moves on to complex programs, he finds them comprised of logical divisions that correspond to our structured paragraphs. A textbook defines these as "a set of units often referred to as 'blocks' or 'modules,'"[1] each of which performs a separate function that are combined to form the program. As the textbook demonstrates in a tree like those you write, a main control module directs a hierarchy of processing modules.

Other similarities are apparent. Each module is complete in itself and is tested separately (as we hope you'll test the internal structure of your body paragraphs in the revision process). Modules are limited in length, each desirably no more than a page of printer output. (We suggest that you restrict your paragraphs to no more than a handwritten page, if that.)

Even more significant are the comments required in the computer program to prepare the human reader. These explanations strongly suggest our previous reminder to stress relationships between sections of your full-length paper:

Comments are used in the program to document the logic. Comments are (a) at the beginning of the program to explain the purpose, structure, and flow of the program; (b) at the beginning of each module to explain the purpose of the module; and (c) in among the program coding lines [comparable to sentences] to explain coding which may not be clear.[2]

The anticipation of the human reader's need to know is one of the factors in what is termed "structured programming," a fairly recent improvement in the field. In Marian Bohl's words, this is "a *philosophy* of writing programs according to a certain set of rules in order to achieve a certain set of objectives" [emphasis hers].[3]

Structured programming, writes Dennie Van Tassel, has three important characteristics:

1. Top-down design
2. Modular programming
3. Structured coding[4]

That philosophy accounts for the success of the program plan, which also emphasizes much the same three characteristics, transferred to the field of human communication. Our version of structured coding will be found in a later chapter, in which we discuss sentences.

First, however, we shall transform the familiar paragraph into a five-paragraph paper.

FROM PARAGRAPH INTO PAPER

As the subject of our illustration of this important process, we shall choose John Fitzgerald Kennedy, the youngest President America has ever elected. We shall rely on general knowledge, the kind of information available to the public.

Our paragraph reads as follows:

> Chief among John Fitzgerald Kennedy's assets was his kindred appeal to the youthful American spirit. As the youngest elected President, at 43 he did not look his age. He was tall and well-built, with a strong yet engaging Irish face. Moreover, he possessed a youthful charisma. He seemed to like all kinds of people, and they warmed to him, both men and women. Most important, he spoke to them of and from the ideals of youth. For Americans, he urged civil rights and labor reform, better medical attention for the aged, altruistic missions abroad. For the world, he pledged an attack against mankind's oldest enemies: tyranny, poverty, disease, and war itself.

The structure tree for that paragraph looks like this (where one item generates one sentence):

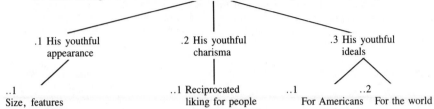

1.0 Chief among JFK's assets was his kindred appeal to the youthful American spirit.

.1 His youthful appearance	.2 His youthful charisma	.3 His youthful ideals

..1 Size, features

..1 Reciprocated liking for people

..1 For Americans ..2 For the world

1. Chief among the assets that JFK brought to the White House was his kindred appeal to the youthful American spirit.
   .1 As the youngest elected president, at 43 he did not look his age.
   ..1 He was tall and well-built, with a strong yet engaging Irish face.
   .2 Moreover, he possessed a youthful charisma.
   ..1 He seemed to like all kinds of people, and they warmed to him, both men and women.
   .3 Most important, he spoke to them of and from the ideals of youth.
   ..1 For Americans, he urged civil rights and labor reform, better medical attention for the aged, altruistic missions abroad.
   ..2 For the world, he pledged an attack against mankind's oldest enemies: tyranny, poverty, disease, and war itself.

You probably find that in this paragraph too many ideas are introduced and then dropped without exploration. The three main points are cramped together, despite the disparity of their topics. Clearly, better judgment suggests that the material be expanded in order to allot each point more adequate discussion. We shall expand the structure chart as follows, retaining the already broad cover statement.

1.0 Chief among JFK's assets was his kindred appeal to the youthful American spirit.

1. His youthful appearance	.2 His youthful charisma	.3 His dedication to youthful ideals

..1 In build   ..2 In features

..1 His liking for people   ..2 Their response

..1 For Americans   ..2 For the world

Selfless ness   Peace Corps   Pledge   Treaty

1.0 Chief among JFK's assets was his kindred appeal to the youthful American spirit.

.1 As the youngest elected president, at 43 he did not look his age. ..1 In build, he was tall and compact, well-proportioned and muscular after a privileged upbringing that stressed athletic competition in tennis, sailboating, and the Kennedys' specialty, touch-football. ..2 His features were engagingly Irish, his tanned face strong and unlined, set off by good teeth and abundant unruly brown hair that showed no gray. ..3 His emphasis on physical fitness inspired schools all over the country to set up training programs and achievement standards for young people.

.2 Moreover, he possessed a youthful charisma. ..1 He seemed genuinely to like all people, both as individuals and in groups. His speeches, presented with a sure poise that was seasoned with fervor and enthusiasm, invariably won their approval. ..2 They warmed to see him romp with the Kennedy children; women responded to his sex appeal. Yet he was a man's man, a twice-decorated Navy hero who had saved his crew from disaster and death.

.3 Most important of all, he thought and spoke the ideals of youth. ..1 He asked Americans to put selfish personal interests behind them and to rally around basic human values: civil rights, labor reform, medical attention for the elderly. "Ask not what your country can do for you," he urged. "Ask what you can do for your country." Through the Peace Corps, he inspired American young people to undertake missions of good will as individual ambassadors to disadvantaged countries. ..2 He looked beyond America to the world, pledging an attack on the enemies of all men: tyranny, poverty, disease, and war itself. Having faced down the Soviets twice, he won his strongest bid for peace in 1963, when the United States, Great Britain, and the Soviet Union signed the Nuclear Test-Ban Treaty.

As you see, the same outline can produce both a single paragraph and a paper of several paragraphs. The difference lies in the number of details that you bring to your topic.

INTRODUCTIONS

A much-repeated rule for writing goes like this: In the introduction, you say what you're going to say. In the body, you say it. In the conclusion, you say what you have said. Like all trite advice, this one has considerable validity, or it wouldn't have become trite.

The trick is to relay the message each time in different words. As we continue to remind you, the big danger in writing by a pattern is that you'll lapse into thoughtless repetition. To write a good introduction is not easy. Most people find it the most difficult phase of the composing process. You may want to consider these suggestions.

1. Everybody agrees that it is hard to get started. The longest book may start with but a single sentence, but that sentence often produces all kinds of difficulties. One solution is simply to delay. Write anything that seems halfway possible, just so long as you end the paragraph with your cover statement. Then, after you've written the body of the paper and the conclusion, come back to the introduction and re-work those first sentences. At this stage, you are full of the facts you have presented: you have arrived at your personal rhythm of writing. Thus, your introduction will reflect the essay as a whole in tone, diction, and structure, as it may not if you struggle to complete it before you write the body.

2. If your paper is concerned with a discussion of some author's work (as in English papers), you should refer to it in the first or second sentence. Don't use an entire sentence to convey that simple fact. Introductions should be full of helpful facts that prepare your reader for the material in the paper. Unless the paper is quite long—or unless it is a professional report—it is simply repetitious to review all that you will shortly be saying.

Most paperbacks have information about the author or the given work on the back cover. Such information—presented in your own words—provides a good send-off.

3. Don't begin with your thesis. If you do, you will feel the need to come back to it as you conclude the introduction; thus, that paragraph becomes circular and repetitious.

4. The simplest introduction is a matter of the numerical reduction: *Most* authorities say so-and-so. *Some* claim such-and-such. *This one,* however ... And then your cover sentence.

Consider the implications of this real-life situation.

> Bruce Howard is an older graduate student at the University. Although he is in the MBA program, he meets part of his expenses by grading freshman English papers. Thus far in the semester, he has not yet learned the individual students in the four classes for which he grades.
>
> As he crosses campus this morning, he's feeling particularly over-burdened and harassed. Ahead of him are two tests in his own field.
>
> A girl's voice hails him. "Oh, Mr. Howard! Wait—Please wait a minute!"
>
> A small, average-looking girl in jeans dashes up, panting. "I left out a big chunk of my paper yesterday!" she gasps out, and then stands waiting.
>
> Bruce wrests his mind away from statistics. He can't place the girl at all. Which class? Which paper? Each of the four groups has just handed in assignments.
>
> "Use your head," he says grimly. "Tell me which class you're in. What your name is. What you wrote about. *Then* refer to what you left out!"

In such a situation, you can see that a general-to-specific supply of facts is required: Of Bruce's eighty students, he needs to know which particular class of twenty; of these twenty students, this one girl's name; of the various topics, this particular topic.

A better approach would have developed this way: "I'm in the fourth-period class. My name is Betty Smith. In my paper on food additives, I left out the fourth page ..."

From the general to the specific—again it's obvious that this is the order in which our minds best accept facts. Your reader, unlike Bruce, will not be torn away from his own concerns; he is most likely to be reading at his own convenience. Still, it is only courtesy to introduce your subject with a few preliminary steps that convey him politely from his former thoughts to yours. You'll find it helpful to think of your discussion as a small world, like the world of the play that you go to see performed in an amphitheater. Just as steps lead down into that world of the drama, so the sentences of the introduction gradually direct the reader into the world of your thoughts.

Here is an example of a general-to-specific introduction suitable for the Kennedy paper.

> In orchestrating favorable publicity, John Fitzgerald Kennedy's victorious campaign for President has never been equalled. Junketing around the country in his father's 40-passenger Convair, he and his attractive, lively family constantly magnetized newsmen: making speeches, hosting VIPs, attending meetings, visiting homes and hospitals. Perhaps the most effective strategy for attention flowered in the Kennedy-Nixon TV debates, a single one of which attracted an estimated hundred million viewers. All this visibility made clear the chief asset that swept Kennedy to the White House: the appeal of his youthful vigor to those Americans whom he led to "think young."

Note that the first statement is very broad: Of all the presidential campaigns, this one managed to evoke the most successful response from the news media. In the second sentence, the subject—the campaigners as a body—is limited to the Kennedys, and the predicate (attracting news coverage) becomes more explicitly a matter of creating a persona, followed by references to specific classes of activity. The third sentence further limits both subject and focus to John Kennedy and the famous TV debates. The fourth sentence finally singles out a quality of success made obvious to the public by all this exposure.

Desirably, the general to specific introduction supplies a number of broad facts that the later discussion will not repeat. Its intention is to catch the reader's attention, while providing a basis for the material to come. The careful writer avoids overlapping statements, particularly those that simply restate what has already been said. As an example, examine the following paragraph, prepared by a student whose paper discusses three main characteristics of Eve.

> In Milton's *Paradise Lost,* the personality of Eve makes her an excellent candidate for the initiation of the plot of the destruction of mankind. Her character renders Eve the better target for Satan because her qualities offer the most promise for a successful completion of his plan. Eve's vain, ambitious, jealous nature makes it impossible for her to either resist the temptation presented by Satan or to prevent Satan from delivering ruin to herself and Adam.

You will note that in each sentence Eve's qualities are mentioned, as is Satan's plot.

(Note also that the thesis is confused, seeming to promise to prove the two infinitives that conclude the sentence, and that the use of *herself* is incorrect.)

Here are some variations of the general-to-specific introduction that work well, without being difficult. (The tone of these introductions does not necessarily accord with the elegiac tone of the five-paragraph Kennedy essay.)

A Relevant Quotation

You may direct an additional beam of light on your subject by opening with a suitable quotation, providing that it is pertinent. If you are discussing a literary work, for example, the quotation might come from that work or from something that deals with the same subject. Avoid sweeping generalizations or old sayings. (By now, everybody knows that all the world loves a lover!) A quotation may be defined as a specific statement made by an identifiable person.

> "When certain historic ideas in the life of the nation had to be clarified," said Franklin Delano Roosevelt, "all great Presidents were leaders of thought." At the time of Kennedy's presidential campaign, the social reform movement that erupted later in the Sixties was already germinating. Just ahead lay the upheaval of campus unrest, the proliferation of various dissention groups, newly voiced concern for the rights of the individual who opposed the majority. Because this building idealism was largely nurtured by a spiritual optimism typically American, the chief asset that swept Kennedy to the White House was the appeal of his youthful vigor to those Americans he led to "think young."

Comparison/Contrast

You may set up some logical association in the introduction like comparison/contrast or cause/effect. The initial two sentences may state the first factor; the thesis anticipates the second, which the body of the paper will demonstrate.

> When John Fitgerald Kennedy—a practicing Catholic—decided to run for President, many Democrats remembered the dismal failure in 1928 of the country's only other Catholic candidate, Al Smith. Beyond their religion, however, the image projected by each man affected the voters in sharp contrast. Smith was a wise-cracking, hard-nosed product of the slums, whose accent, cocked derby hat, and questionable friendships continued to remind voters of his slums background. Conversely, the Kennedys' wealth, education, and polish—acquired in two generations—reminded voters that the levels of the social ladder could be made to disappear behind the climber. Where the Catholic Al Smith had failed at the polls, the Catholic JFK succeeded; the negative factor of his religion was outweighed by the charisma that enabled voters to "think young."

A Question

You may raise a question—or more than one—that you will answer immediately, either in the body of the paper, or in the conclusion.

> What were the sources of Kennedy's personal popularity as a Presidential candidate? The country seemed to seek a leader, and from childhood Kennedy had been trained to lead. He had been a leader in the country's top schools; he had learned about leadership as a member of Congress, and then as a Senator. His war record also made him a hero; his book had won a Pulitzer Prize. He had optimistic answers for the country's problems; he had the power of wealth behind him. The chief asset that brought him to the White House, however, was the appeal of his youthful vigor to those he led to "think young."

Strawman or Contrast

You can set up a strawman—a simplistic suggestion or concept that your paper will disprove. Suppose that your thesis urges the maintainance of strict regulations on the disposal of nuclear waste. Then your introduction might suggest blandly that we reactivate the plan of piling all nuclear waste in a hole, where it will destroy itself—if it doesn't all leak away first.

If such a satiric tone does not suit your subject, you can modify the same beginning to present some notion that is commonly held—and then rebut it. (Example: Speech is entirely learned behavior.)

> The wiseacres of the late 1950s swore that John Kennedy would never become President. A man who simply ignored the party bosses—how could he land the Democratic nomination? Why, he didn't have a single top leader in his corner. No one really important was behind him except his father. All that gladhanding around the country wouldn't count for anything where the Big Boys were concerned.

> But, of course, that gladhanding did the job. For, in winning local Democratic leaders to his corner, Kennedy knew they'd pressure the party big-wigs. The local leaders fell under the sway of that chief asset that brought Kennedy to the White House—the appeal of his youthful vigor to those whom he led to "think young."

Like the often-used anecdote to snare the reader's attention, the strawman lead-in usually requires an extra paragraph for its development.

Weaknesses to Avoid in Writing Introductions

1. Don't make your introduction too long. Three or four good, full sentences are ample for a paper of four handwritten pages. The body of your essay is the equivalent of the featured speech of an after-dinner speaker. Your introduction parallels the *few* well-chosen words with which the emcee presents the chief speaker. How do you feel if the introducer rambles on and on?

2. Don't go off at a tangent. Your sentences should lead to that thesis statement; that's their reason for being.

3. Don't promise more than you can deliver. By all means, write strongly. But don't raise the umbrella of your cover sentence so high over a relatively few facts that it's blown inside out!

CONCLUSIONS

Like introductions, conclusions serve specific purposes, chief of which is to hammer home the thought of the paper—now that you've explained and supported that thought. You should express a tone of finality. In effect, you put your arm around your reader's shoulders and say with utmost confidence: "Now that you've understood these excellent arguments, of course you agree with my thesis. Thanks for reading, and farewell."

If you used the general-to-specific form of introduction, you may simply reverse its descending steps into an ascent, moving from the world of your thought up to the reader's real world again. Such a conclusion might read like this:

> After Kennedy's death, most of his plans for conquering the New Frontier of social change remained unrealized. The appeal to the country's basic values and ideals that had been generated by his vigor, his charm, his rhetoric, now dissolved into the bickering conflicts of the tumultous Sixties. Without its leader, the quest that began in Camelot ended, and its visionaries subsided into the Me Generation.

In addition, you may acknowledge any rebuttal of your points that the reader might consider. Or you may refer to some significant fact that does not fit into the body of your paper. Because the three main points of the Kennedy paper are tightly constructed, for example, they offer no opportunity to inform the reader that, behind Kennedy's appearance of youthful vigor, lay an astonishing number of serious health problems he had been taught to ignore.

The conclusion is also the place for a final touch of irony. After reference to the big plane that Joe Kennedy prcvided for the family's public appearances, you might observe that the elder Kennedy proved to be a handicap to his son's campaign and a particularly delicate problem.[5]

Much like the devices that enrich an introduction, the following variations of the conclusion prove to be effective.

Asking a Question

It is often good strategy to ask a question, for by doing so you take a last opportunity to involve the reader. Most people respond to a challenge, even if very briefly.

> More than twenty years have passed since Americans responded to Kennedy's vitality, his leadership, his assurances that together they could right many of the world's wrongs. As recently as 1976, a Gallup poll ranked Kennedy among the three greatest presidents, ahead even of Lincoln. Now, however, as economic complexities diminish the people's concern for the idealism he preached, authorities examine his record in the sharper light of actual accomplishments. Just as Eisenhower's status has been virtually reversed—from weak to strong—so Kennedy's ratings have slipped with the fading of his personal impact.

Tie with Introduction

You may bring your introduction full-circle by alluding to whatever device you used there: If you asked a question, you should answer it; if you set up a strawman, you may wittily disparage it.

> Thus, Kennedy's chief asset—his altruistic appeal from youth to youth—outweighed voters' fears that a Catholic President would jeopardize the separation

of church and state. Kennedy's openness in discussing the subject, his reiteration that his first concern would be his Presidential Oath, helped to allay the questions raised by his opponents. While he put down one bogey, however, other restrictions continue to limit candidates for America's highest office, and few could bring with them Kennedy's plethora of assets.

Revealing Additional Information

The conclusion is the place for a "clincher." Because the Kennedy paper is based on the youthful vitality conveyed by the President, the fact that such vitality was often the result of sheer determination is especially effective as a conclusion.

> Thus, a dominant factor in Kennedy's success was his appeal to and from youth—to young Americans as well as to the youthful spirit in those over thirty, from his own vital force. Unknown to the public, that energy often stemmed from sheer determination. Kennedy had been a sickly child and, as an adult, continued to suffer from serious health problems. He underwent three long operations on his spine that kept him in bed for months and in continuing pain. He was subject to malarial attacks; he had Addison's disease and its accompanying loss of immunity to infections. With his medical records sealed, and with the Kennedys' disdain of physical weakness, he conveyed an unquenchable vitality that earned him his father's set goal and the country's highest honor.[6]

Looking Ahead

Readers generally enjoy having the life of some famous person in the past weighed against the values of today. "What if?" is one of the best questions to ask—and answer—in preparing a concusion.

> Like the figures in a Greek frieze, the public image of Kennedy remains unchanged—young, assured, vital, grandly promising leadership to right the wrongs of the world. Would those components of his person have lasted as he aged? Probably so, for he had always looked younger than his years. As a new Congressman, he appeared to be a skinny undergraduate, and, at 43, he seemed no more than 35. The charismatic warmth and humor, the quick, determined mind were similarly built into his genes. As for the New Frontier he envisioned, even there he might have won success, for after McCarthyism the country was ripe for change. Had Kennedy lived, the record that historians now deem scanty might well have weighted history.

Any of these possibilities may be combined. Here are some weaknesses to avoid:

1. Don't just stop, or cut the reader off abruptly.
2. Don't be repetitious. Find synonyms and alternate phrasings.
3. Don't go on and on. Three or four sentences are enough.

SUMMARY

The relationship of the programmed paragraph to the full-length paper is much like that of the scale model some architects construct before the actual building process.

In learning the paragraph, you have followed their example. While the architect's scale model soon retires as a mere curiosity, however, the programmed paragraph you have mastered continues to serve your basic writing needs. In maintaining the clarity of the full-length paper, you depend on it to guide each body paragraph's internal structure.

The general-to-specific descent required by the algorithm can be likened to a brief flight of stairs, first in the scale model and then in the actual building. The steps descending from the rear portico to the driveway bear the same relationship to each other, whether measured in inches or in feet. The relationship of the cover sentence to its main supports to their minor supports is much the same, whether in a ten-sentence paragraph or a hundred-sentence paper. The success of your overall organization depends upon your remembering that.

ASSIGNMENTS

1. In the introductory and concluding paragraphs of the Kennedy paper, work out the descent from general to specific. In each paragraph, underline the words that carry forward the thought that is being developed, that is, the idea in the introduction that narrows, and the idea in the conclusion that opens outward.

2. If you know the Adam-Eve story in Genesis, rewrite the student paragraph given earlier.

3. Work out a structure tree about the life of someone you know well. Then prepare an introduction and a conclusion suitable for writing such a paper.

4. Plan a comparison/contrast paper around one of the following titles (or one of your own). Design a structure tree and then write the introductory paragraph that would suit its topic.

> A Contrast between a Job and a Career
> Differences in Parenting in a One-Parent Household
> Comparable "Perks" Available in Two Different Careers
> Comparison of Eastern and Western Square-Dancing
> Differences in Tennis and Racquetball
> Differences Found in One School District and Another

5. For each kind of introduction illustrated earlier, write an opening sentence that would be suitable for it (excepting the form you employed in 4).

NOTES

1. Gordon B. Davis, *Introduction to Computers* (New York: McGraw Hill, 1977), pp. 119-120.
2. Davis, pp. 127-128.

3. Marilyn Bohl, *A Guide for Programmers* (Englewood Cliffs, N.J.: Prentice-Hall, Inc., 1978), p. 138.

4. Dennie Van Tassel, *Program Style, Design, Efficiency, Debugging and Testing,* 2nd ed. (Englewood Cliffs, N.J.: Prentice-Hall, Inc. 1978), p. 62.

5. This ironic fact is thoroughly explored in Herbert Parmet's engrossing biography, *Jack: The Struggles of John Kennedy* (New York: Dial Press, 1980).

6. Parmet carefully supports the details of Kennedy's recurring illnesses and the family's efforts to keep them from the public.

6
DEVELOPING
THE SENTENCE

GOAL: To learn the kinds of subordination and their benefits to sentence structure

In discussing written communication so far, we have emphasized the need for organization of paragraph and paper, emphasizing the interests of clarity.

As we have mentioned, to adhere to a pattern in writing may result in a wooden sameness of expression. If we lose sight of other necessities, our facts may march forth stolidly to the same drumbeat, not sufficiently differentiated to maintain the reader's attention.

What is needed to enliven and individualize such writing? Variation in sentence structure and the resulting rhythms; the selection of colorful words; an attention to tone—in good writing these concerns stand next to clarity.

At this stage, the sentence as a separate entity becomes our focus. Without venturing into the arid areas of grammar, we shall investigate the advantages of subordination—the variations provided by clauses and phrases. We shall consider means of heightening their impact, as in right- and left-branching sentences, and the devices of parallelism and balance.

SUBORDINATION

Many people find it stressful to put facts down on paper—the right facts in the right places, spelled correctly and set off by the right punctuation, and all the rest. Consequently, students' sentence structure often reflects only basic relationships—much the same, incidentally, as the programmer employs for the computer:

this *and* this
this *not* that
this *or* that
this *but* that
if this, *then* that
this *while* that

As a result, their sentence structure turns out to be somewhat limited. Among students who are quick to say that writing is not their bag, the tendency is to produce choppy single clauses, or two main clauses hobbled by coordinating conjunctions (*and, but,* and the *or* brothers—*or, for,* and *nor).*

A.   The Wife of Bath is a lusty woman. She is smart and rich and high-spirited. She likes men and they like her. The Wife is not intimidated by men; indeed, she surpasses them. In her opinion, wise women should follow her example.

You'll remember that in chapter two a famous cryptographer warned us of the human tendency to fall into patterns, even when we intend to avoid them. The student who sets out to use better structure than the example above often elects a pattern that is surprisingly common: a single subject and two finite verbs—again linked by coordinating conjunctions:

B.   The *Lou Grant Show* was five years old and sinking in the ratings. But all the CBS Monday night shows were down and feeling the effects of ABC's *Monday Night Football. . . .* The show replacing *Lou Grant* had even poorer ratings last spring and came up with only a 22 share in its first four showings last spring.

While these sentences provide more details than the first student's, they do not represent subordination. Perhaps neither writer understands the term.

Subordination is the quiet art of signaling the reader that one portion of a sentence—the main clause—is more important than the rest. It indicates that importance by linking to the main clause as *lesser* elements any condition, time, or place element that binds it, as well as appropriate minor details limited in structure and number of syllables.

The hierarchy of subordination goes like this:

sentence
main clause
dependent clause
phrase
word

In college-level writing, a main clause can be considered as having certain slots before and after it. (We advise against interrupting the subject and its verb other than very briefly. Together they convey the thrust of the message.) Thus, a slot precedes the main clause that is available for a dependent clause or one of the various kinds of phrases. Similar availabilities follow the main clause, including that useful noun phrase, the appositive. Each of these may carry a thought that, without subordination, would wastefully require an entire sentence (as in example A, above).

Note: An important exception is the statement of a main point or some similar general statement. Such sentences should remain simple and direct, not only to avoid confusing the reader with details, but as a means of contrast and therefore identification.

Subordination becomes a matter of two groups of words, dependent clauses and phrases. For some of our readers, their varieties may not be immediately available. The next section of this chapter, then, will name and briefly differentiate them. If such terminology is already familiar to you, you may still find our binary definitions decidedly useful.

Definitions

Here again are the elements of a sentence, ranged from most to least importance, as you learned them in elementary school:

> sentence
> main clause
> dependent clause
> phrase
> word

Can you still define them and differentiate between them? Then what are the underlined words in the following sentences?

1. Bill limped slowly toward her, his injured arm supported by a sling.
2. The game having begun, we took our seats.

If a sentence must have a subject and a verb, why aren't the underlined words a sentence? Each one has a subject and a verb.

Are they subordinate clauses? A main clause can stand alone, but a dependent clause can't. These groups of words cannot.

Let's hold off a minute and consider more dependable rules. Ours have the added advantage of being *binary;* everything is one or the other, like the number system that made possible the computer. (A psychologist has said that we work out the answers to most questions on that basis—yes-no; true-false, on-off.) Because a choice of two rules is easier to remember than additional possibilities, we urge you to keep these guides in mind:

> All groups of associated words are either clauses or phrases.
> Everything that is not a clause is a phrase.

What about the sentence? What about a traditional rule: A sentence is a group of words that expresses a complete thought? A more contemporary definition says that a main clause and a sentence can be defined alike. What is the difference, after all, between the words underlined in these examples?

3. <u>Rain fell</u>.
4. When the monsoons arrived, <u>rain fell</u> in leaden-gray sheets all day every day, turning fields into lakes and streams into torrents.

Sentences can support many modifiers—but so can a main clause. Both share the same minimum requirements, a subject and a finite verb.

(A finite verb is a verb that you, as a native speaker, recognize as one that could serve as the main verb for a sentence.)

Here are dependable definitions for a clause and a phrase:

Clause: A clause is a group of associated words that has *both* a subject and a finite verb.
Phrase: A phrase is a group of associated words that does not have *both* a subject and a finite verb.

The two key words here are *both* and *finite*. If you omit *finite,* then you no longer possess the key to determining the status of those underlined words in our previous sentences 1 and 2. They are phrases, not clauses; extremely useful to writers, they are known as *nominative absolutes*.

The word *both* is even more important, for a phrase can *be* a subject, that is, a noun and its modifers:

the two winning American players

It can also be a finite verb:

had been waiting

Unlike phrases, then, both kinds of clauses are alike in possessing a subject and a finite verb. Then how does a dependent (or subordinate) clause differ from a main clause?

A dependent clause is "crippled" by a preceding *subordinator* so that it cannot stand alone. Again, you as a native speaker would not accept it as a sentence:

before I heard him   whoever asks
when she came by   that I knew
although it rained   which is different

(One exception exists, a form that you are unlikely to hear or to use: <u>Had I but known,</u> our friendship would not have lasted. We suggest that you concentrate on the usual requirement of a subordinator.)

A subordinator can be either a subordinating conjunction or a relative pronoun. Close to thirty subordinating conjunctions are available. Some, like *after, as, before, until,* can also be prepositions. *That* often presents difficulties, for it can serve three purposes:

subordinating conjunction:	That I knew him made little difference.
relative pronoun:	He climbed the tree that stood nearest the water.
demonstrative pronoun:	That girl over there can sing.

Moreover, *that* as a conjunction can simply be understood (as in the imperative sentence: [you] Ask me some other time.)

> He told Jean (that) he'd like to know her better.

It is useful to know you can make any main clause into a noun clause by prefacing it with *that*.

> Many computer crimes are never discovered.
> That many computer crimes are never discovered is a disturbing fact of this age of technology.

You'll find this fact helpful in writing the exercises at the end of this chapter.

Subordinators that are relative pronouns introduce adjective or noun clauses. With the exception of *that* (again), they all begin with *wh—: who, which, what, whom, whose* (all but the last-named may add—*ever*).

With this reminder of terms we learned long ago, let us direct our attention to the specifics of subordination. The most important subordinate element is the dependent clause.

Dependent Clauses

Three kinds of dependent clauses exist: adverbial, adjective, and noun. Each carries out the function of its namesake part of speech.

The adverbial clause most often begins or ends the main clause. Its subordinator may suggest a condition imposed on the main clause:

> Although television in Japan and Germany comes with full-stereo, two-track sound, in this country the FCC must first determine a number of patent claims and the resulting license fees.
> Because robots will take over the tedious stages, humans will be freed for more challenging jobs.
> The students showed marked reactions as they considered how the change would affect them.
> When Halley's comet appears in 1985, few Americans will see it.

Adjective clauses are easily recognized because they are attached to a noun:

> The decision that he made was binding.
> The doping process, which results in silicon's ability to conduct current, will eventually be performed by the computer.

Noun clauses most often act as subject or object:

> That she changed her mind was foolish.
> We all wondered what motivated him to change jobs.

Most dependent clauses add more syllables than a corresponding phrase, thus subtly altering the sentence rhythm. Because they could make a complete statement (in many cases) with the subordinator removed, to voice a fact as a dependent clause is to evaluate it as almost equal to the main clause.

An indication of their near-equality is found in the field of artificial intelligence, specifically those studies in which researchers seek to create systems that will translate text from one natural language to another. At least one such system equates dependent clauses with main clauses on a basic level (although differentiated later). In *Artificial Intelligence,* Earl B. Hunt writes:

> The clause, rather than the sentence, is the dependent unit of thought. That is, it eventually translates into an expression in the data base [the structured collection of related information], although it may be an expression contained within another expression.[1]

What this computer analogy suggests for careful writers, then, is that dependent clauses are vehicles for material essential to the meaning of the sentence, as in the following:

> Where he has gone is a mystery.
> I asked what she intended to do.
> They told me that John wanted to marry Betty.
> As the Komodo dragon appeared in the clearing, the tethered goat began to bleat.
> While he is studying, I won't disturb him.
> I believe (that) he intended to go home.

Phrases

Phrases most often serve the useful purpose of expressing necessary information in the fewest possible words. The term *phrase* simpy means a headword and whatever is tied to it: dressed is a verb; had been dressed is a verb phrase. A noun phrase consists of the noun and its modifiers.

Aside from these two, phrases are as follows:

prepositional (a preposition and its noun)	The fan in the case is an antique. At a moment's notice she could be ready. They ran toward the fire.
participial (the word in a verb phrase that carries meaning, either present or past tense; plus its complement)	Entering the lobby, we stayed together. Having once been burned, she was careful. Hugh, separated from the group, felt scared. The colt galloping down the field is mine. The car had departed, leaving us behind. She was tired, worn out from the long day.

gerund	Programming a computer is challenging.
(an -ing verb that acts as a noun,	My favorite sport is sailing.
plus complement)	For speaking to the queen, she was fired.
infinitive	To ask questions is to indicate interest.
(the infinite marker to and a verb	He asked me to serve coffee.
plus complement)	She began to dance madly.
absolute	The sun having set, the Moslems could eat.
(subject and participle or	His gun in his hand, he slipped out.
adjective)	Peggy, her hands pressed to her throat, sobbed out her story.
	She asked John to leave, the hour being over.

Of these, professional writers most often make use of noun phrases (as appositives to rename a subject or object); participial phrases (to introduce action in place of simple adjectives); and the nominative absolute (an entire main clause that has had its finite verb adjusted).

A word about prepositional phrases, before we leave this section. They are prone to overuse. Often they pile up at the end of a sentence; it is desirable to limit them in that case to three. Usually, at least one can be changed to a possessive noun.

For prolific writers, these various forms probably appear without effort, though they may require pruning and shaping at the revision stage.

For beginning writers unused to subordination, it is unwise to stop at every sentence to ask, "Shall I voice this thought as a dependent clause, or as a phrase?" Such decisions will wreck the forward drive of their thoughts, as well as their natural rhythm. For them, too, the changes should come in revision. As they work with the different elements, they will find themselves increasingly comfortable with the various structures, until eventually they become natural.

BUILDING EFFECTIVE SENTENCES

With your memory of clauses and phrases renewed, we can discuss some elements of good writing practice to which they contribute: specifically right- and left-branching sentences.

In organizing paragraph and paper thus far, our development has followed the natural order of perception—from the "whole" to its parts, from the top down. Such progress has its parallel at the level of the sentence. The main clause is equivalent to the cover sentence, followed by a dependent clause or phrase that focuses on some detail of it; in turn, a detail in the second level appears in the third, and so on. Such a sentence is said to be right-branching (as opposed to left-branching, in which the main clause is preceded by phrases or a dependent clause).

It is also said to be "cumulative"; the main clause is underlined by a succession of added details.

The cumulative sentence is neatly parallelled by a sequence of camera shots long customary in television.

Imagine the sign-on of NBC's *Today* show when Jane Pauley will be host. We first see a "long" shot of the group of regulars with her in the middle. The camera then singles her out in a "mid" shot, waist high. When she begins to speak, the view changes to a close-up and, as she introduces the news, her words become pictured thought.

TODAY SHOW

Long shot:	The entire set—people, desk, background
Mid-shot:	Jane from the waist up: the desk
Close-up:	Jane's face
Detail:	Illustrations of her words

CUMULATIVE SENTENCE

Long shot:	The Wife of Bath was a remarkable traveller,
Mid-shot:	having journeyed three times to the Holy Land
Close-up:	by ship and on horseback,
Detail:	riding astride like a man.

The "downshifts" do not require any special order in their grammatical elements. Thus, in the second level above, the participial phrase clarifies the preceding general statement. The third level refers to the mode of travel in paired prepositional phrases, and the specific fourth appears as a participial phrase.

The narrowing of the focus is represented in the following examples by indentation. As you will see, similar indentations that are used in what is termed "structured" programming also represent relationships in the levels of coding.

    A. Colonial courting was a long ordeal,
           involving the permission of both sets of parents,
               who attended to matters of finance
                 before the suitor proposed.

Here, *involving* (etc.) tells what kind of ordeal in a participial phrase; *who attended* refers to both sets of parents in an adjective clause; *before . . . proposed* tells when they *attended* to money matters, an adverbial clause.

    B. GM car designers spend hours in their wind tunnel,
          a multi-million dollar construction
             that makes possible aerodynamic tests
               intended to reduce the car's air drag.

In this sentence the second level is a noun phrase used as an appositive (it rewords *wind tunnel);* the third level is an adjective clause that explains *construction;* the fourth level is a participial phrase that modifies *tests.*

  C. A computer is easily programmed to play ticktacktoe,
    needing only a "perfect" algorithm
      that will find a forced win
        if it exists.

The cumulative sentence offers many advantages to the careful writer—readability, conciseness, texture. In addition, it can achieve good sentence rhythm, a subject we discuss later.

Readability

Obviously, since the cumulative sentence reflects our algorithm within the limits of the single sentence, it presents information as the reader can best comprehend it. You remember that the algorithm's progressive descent is rendered visible in just such indentations of those of examples A, B, and C above. Similar indentations in good programming bear out the analogy of the programmer and the writer. Van Tassel urges program designers to clarify logical relationships visually, inasmuch as future human readers must review their work. His book, *Program Style, Design, Efficiency, Debugging, and Testing,* includes a contrast between unstructured programming (a long unindented list) and structured programming. Structured programming closely resembles the traditional formal outline for an essay, as evidenced in the following brief segment:[2]

  (1) IF p THEN
     A function
     B function
  (2) IF q then
    (3) IF t then
       G function
     (4)DOWHILE u
        H function
     (4) ENDDO
       I function
    (3) (ELSE)
    (3) ENDIF
  (2) ELSE

For writers prone to long sentences, cumulative sentences offer a necessary clarity that might otherwise be absent. Composition teachers generally urge students to write long sentences, probably to avoid such main-clause patterns as our earlier examples. Moreover, a number of reading-comprehension studies establish that college-level readers understand sentences of a length that the high school-level reader would find difficult. Ergo, it behooves college-level writers to match the ability of their expected audience.

  Not just in student writing but in bureaucratic directive as well, a fondness for long sentences often results in communication no more successful than a flopover television picture. The cumulative sentence, by contrast, is admittedly long (the Hemingway example we quote below has 73 words!); yet, because it is broken up in meaningful, breath-sized pieces, when well handled it possesses both life and logic.

Conciseness

Because the cumulative sentence depends on subordination, it supplies facts with a minimum of wasted syllables. (The syllable, rather than the word, is the unit for measuring length.) Suppose we were to express the thoughts presented in example B (above) as might the student who wrote about the Wife of Bath:

> Colonial courting was an ordeal.
> It involved not only the young people, but also both sets of parents.
> First, the parents arranged the couple's finances among themselves.
> Then the suitor was given permission to propose.

Instead of the twenty-four words found in the cumulative sentence, individual sentences require a total of thirty-two words. (Simple sentences like these, however, are well suited to difficult material or to a process, the steps of which need to be grasped individually.)

For the writer who must deal with a given subject on a fairly general level, the cumulative sentence makes possible the use of specific details and personal comment that, in separate sentences, would represent digression.

Writing on some subject other than grammatical terms, for example, an essayist might well pause to explain his allusion to the term *modifier* in one sentence, thus:

> To modify a word is to restrict its meaning,
> a paradox whereby you subtract from its application
> by adding to it specific details
> that enlarge upon your thought.

Texture

While cumulative sentences are hardly new, it was Francis Christensen of the University of Southern California who created the term and enlarged on its ability to improve the texture of writing. By its very form, he points out in *Notes for a New Rhetoric* (1967), the cumulative sentence invites details that promote richness and variety of structure.

Such sentences provide a vehicle for managing a variety of difficult writing situations. Consider the sports writer at the winter Olympics, who must match words to a skier's swooping descent of a mountain. Does he turn to a series of short sentences, the customary device for handling action? Yet the jerky rhythm of short sentences can hardly do credit to that ongoing express-train descent.

See what Hemingway devises:

> George was coming down in the telemark position,
>   kneeling,
>   one leg forward and bent,
>   the other trailing,
>   his sticks hanging like some insect's thin legs,
>   kicking up puffs of snow, and finally,
> the whole kneeling, trailing figure coming around in a
> beautiful right curve,
>   crouching,
>   the legs shot forward and back,
>   the body leaning out against the swing,
>   the sticks accenting the curve like points of light,
> all in a wild cloud of snow.[3]

Seventy-three words—and yet few of us would complain of its wordiness.

The number of levels in a cumulative sentence need not always be four, or even three. For the non-professional, four is a good place to stop. In "The Bear," Falkner manages twelve—each one very long!

The Left-Branching Sentence

In filling the slot that precedes the main clause of a sentence, the careful writer thinks to himself: Now, my reader doesn't yet know the principal thought—my reason for voicing this sentence. Thus, I should avoid a long participial phrase that so far has nothing to modify; the reader cannot process such information unless my paragraph is obviously about a single subject.

On the other hand, the slot preceding the main clause is ideal for any conditions that control or contribute to the main clause—especially adverbial clauses that begin with *although, as, as soon as, because, before, if, when,* and so on.

I can also safely include one or two prepositional phrases because of their brevity, especially those that present facts of time and place.

In any event, I should watch the length of introducing subordination, so that it avoids a top-heavy effect when the subsequent main clause is short.

The weaknesses of a left-branching participial phrase are evident in the following passage.

> One reason both men made sacrifices was out of pity. The magician had enough to live on comfortably and could do without the gold he was owed. Loving the knight's wife very dearly and hoping for some miracle that would clear away the black rocks so he could have her, the squire made an even greater sacrifice.

The left-branching sentence is effective in achieving transition between two paragraphs, in that the subordinated material can refer to the subject just discussed, while the main clause looks forward to the new material.

Variations of Main Clause Subject

Within the area of sentence structure comes a problem that you may have experienced in writing by pattern: If you are to maintain the same subject throughout a paragraph, how can you avoid dull repetition? While our answer partakes of several headings, arbitrarily we shall present it here.

Three possibilities of disguise are available:

1. The careful use of left-branching sentences
2. Appropriate synonyms for the subject, including the three cases of pronouns
3. Reversal—changing the customary subject-verb-complement order

1. Several varieties of left-branching subordination prove helpful. Prepositional phrases are always possible. While participial phrases may confuse the reader if a new subject is to be introduced, no such confusion arises if the same subject is retained throughout a paragraph. A dependent clause may introduce an entirely different subject, without detracting from the ongoing force of that found in the main clause.

Ex.: Because evil spirits might come in the night, Joan hid the witchery book in the outhouse.

2. Synonyms always work well, including pronouns.

> The programmer ... The designer of the program ... The program's writer ... He ... To him, it seems ... His chief consideration ...

3. Reversal—a change in normal sentence order—comes not so much as a device but as a writer's commitment to his subject. Often the word pulled out of its natural order is an adverb of negation, *never* or *not*. At the beginning of the sentence it carries considerably more emphasis than in the middle:

> "Never in my life have I seen such a thing!" declared Ma Grimes, her small brown eyes snapping with indignation.

Compare:

> "I have never seen such a thing in my life!"

In a balanced sentence, both clauses may contain reversal:

> Calm as she appeared to him, inside she was raging.

Compare:

> She was raging inside, (as) calm as she appeared to him.

It is sometimes effective to place the object ahead of the sentence:

> The eventual result he deemed to be worth all his effort.

Compare:

> He deemed the eventual result to be worth all his effort.

Under reversal also appears the *periodic sentence*. Any sentence that is not grammatically complete until it is finished fits under this heading. We think of the periodic sentence as one that deliberately builds suspense in order to keep the reader reading:

> Off to the right in the lonely starlit darkness was a lumpish blackness that could be a man . . .

PARALLELISM AND BALANCE

Parallelism and balance are structural devices of rhetoric that depend on similarity of pattern to emphasize likeness or contrast. In addition to emphasis, they add polish and sophistication.

While both often occur together, we find that parallelism implies repetition of key words, phrases, or dependent clauses. Balance, on the other hand, suggests a likeness in rhythm rather than phrasing. In the work of the fluent writer (or speaker), such aids to emphasis may occur spontaneously, especially if the individual is emotionally involved in his material.

Thus far, your most obvious opportunity for parallelism has occurred in the cover sentence's proof phase. As an example:

> As the supernatural reflection of Odysseus' qualities, Homer represents Athene in three forms: as an all-powerful divinity, as a divinity in human form , and as a divinity in the mind of man.

The three noun phrases are similar in purpose (object of the preposition *as),* in word repetition (*divinity),* and in syllable count (eight, nine, and ten), like the sentence you are reading. A gradual increase in the syllable count of the three phrases conveys a note of finality, like the last note of a musical phrase.

It is usually helpful to repeat the preposition or other form word that sets up the parallelism:

> *in* purpose
> *in* word repetition
> *in* syllable count

Another simple but important opportunity for parallelism comes in emphasizing your main points, or any advantages you are presenting to the reader:

You benefit in the first place by ...
A second benefit by which you profit comes with ...
You gain a third benefit by ...

The inexperienced writer often does not realize the need for stressing the key thoughts of his material. Parallelism is one such means.

If you are classifying a number of situations that apparently differ, you can make the point of their underlying similarity by parallel phrasing. Note how carefully this is achieved by Horace Newcomb in detailing the pattern of order in *Star Trek* episodes:

> In the course of its cruises the *Enterprise* encounters some sort of problem. In some cases, the problem is set up by a specific assignment: to explore an apparently barren planetoid, to visit a delegation from an alien civilization. On other occasions the ship simply encounters an unknown situation: other ships have been attacked, planets have been destroyed, an invasion force is moving toward them. On still other occasions strange things begin to happen aboard the ship: erratic behavior among members of the crew or the command staff, malfunction of some component of the ship.[4]

In such conscious repetition there is strength. Parallelism adds not only emphasis but an imposed order that the reader finds satisfying.

The type of order supplied by balanced sentences is more often a matter of two sentences (or two dependent clauses) that state opposed situations in memorable phrasing. Books of quotations cite hundreds. The *Maxims* of La Rochefoucauld, for example, offer balanced sentences that depend on devices we can utilize ourselves. One of his favorites consists of linking opposites and then pronouncing the same judgment on both: (our translation)

> One is neither so happy nor so miserable as one thinks.

In the next two maxims, the philosopher balances main clauses by repeating all but two or three words:

> We make promises according to our hopes;
>
> we fulfill them according to our fears.
>
> Everyone complains of his memory;
>
> no one complains of his judgment.

The following sentence depends only on if-then logic and a rough similarity of rhythm (three stresses):

> If one judges love by most of its results, it seems more like hatred than affection.

The best way to achieve such sophisticated balance is to work with certain pairs of sentences that oppose or link statements, as in the slots that follow *not—*

rather; neither—nor; both—and; although—yet; not only—but also; because— therefore. The following illustrations were written by students:

> One school of writing stresses self-expression; the other sees its goal as enhanced communication.
>
> Programming is not just writing commands to a computer; rather, it is a long, involved process based on understanding a complex problem.
>
> The would-be computer criminal balances cost against value—time and effort required as opposed to eventual profit.
>
> The security man must also balance cost against value—the high cost of protection against the value of what can be stolen.

In our next chaper we shall progress to the level of words—the right words in the right places for liveliness and effective tone. Because the revision process offers an opportune time for such polishing, we shall discuss it as well.

SUMMARY

Probably the most popular pattern of writing among students and the general public alike is that of main clauses strung together with coordinate conjunctions. Writers interested in improving their style, however, work for subordination. That is, they relate the grammatical form of a detail to its importance in the sentence. Subordination depends on two groups of elements—dependent clauses and phrases. Because all clauses possess both a subject and a finite verb, they are considered more important than corresponding phrases (which do not have both a subject and a finite verb) that possess the value of brevity. Phrases that contain verbs acting as other parts of speech (paticipial, gerund, and infinitive phrases) introduce much-needed action in a sentence. Noun phrases as appositives effectively rename and emphasize an element important to meaning.

If subordination is placed before the main clause, it is said to be left-branching; if after the main clause, it is right-branching or cumulative. Cumulative sentences may replicate the hierarchical steps of the algorithm, for each successive level of descent focuses on some element in the preceding level.

Parallelism and balance offer sophisticated means of stressing relationships between two or more thoughts of equal rank. They depend on similarities of wording and rhythm.

ASSIGNMENTS

1. These additional translations of La Rochefoucauld's maxims were intended to be brief and concise. Adjust them as necessary to restore their crisp balance.

   a. Jealousy is always born with love, but when love dies it doesn't always die with it.

   b. Small passions disappear with absence, like candles extinguished by wind. Yet just as the wind turns a fire into a roaring blaze, so great love is augmented by absence.

   c. Generosity is often no more than the pride of giving, and that which we give we love less than that.

   d. The vanity that we find unbearable in others is that which wounds our own self-love.

   e. It is much easier to know mankind in general than it is to know one man in particular.

2. Link the following short sentences that are grouped together into a single long sentence, as directed.

Ex: ADVERBIAL CLAUSE, PARTICIPIAL PHRASE, MAIN CLAUSE, PARTICIPIAL PHRASE

1. One day I was riding horseback in the desert.
2. I was accompanied by a friend.
3. My horse shied suddenly.
4. It almost unseated me.

> As I was riding horseback in the desert one day, accompanied by a friend, my horse shied suddenly, almost unseating me.

MAIN CLAUSE, RELATIVE CLAUSE, ADVERBIAL CLAUSE

1. The Druids were a Celtic priestly caste.
2. Their name meant "knower of trees."
3. They were associated with a tree cult.

MAIN CLAUSE, ADVERBIAL CLAUSE,
ADJECTIVE (RELATIVE) CLAUSE

1. Oak trees were sacred to them.
2. Mistletoe was, too.
3. It was often found high up in oaks.

MAIN CLAUSE, PARTICIPIAL PHRASE,
NOUN PHRASE AS APPOSITIVE

1. The Druids called it "the golden bough."
2. They believed it was engendered by lightning.
3. Lightning was Thor's thunderbolt.

MAIN CLAUSE, ADVERBIAL CLAUSE, ADVERBIAL CLAUSE

1. Holly trees were important in Druidic rites.
2. They were in later English villages, too.
3. The people elected a "holly boy."

PREPOSITIONAL PHRASE, PREPOSITIONAL PHRASE,
ADVERBIAL CLAUSE, MAIN CLAUSE

1. The day was an early June afternoon.
2. The place was at the club.

3. The crowd around the swimming pool was comprised mostly of women and children.
4. A surprising thing happened.

ADVERBIAL CLAUSE, MAIN CLAUSE,
PARTICIPIAL PHRASE, ADJECTIVE PHRASE

1. Some women watched their youngsters learning to swim.
2. Others were stretched out on recliners.
3. They were reinforcing their tans.
4. They were half asleep in the sun.

A SINGLE ADVERB, MAIN CLAUSE COMBINING 2 AND 3
AS DOUBLE VERB, NOUN PHRASE

1. It happened suddenly.
2. An old jalopy roared up the driveway.
3. It screeched to a halt.
4. It stopped just fifty feet from the pool.

MAIN CLAUSE WITH DOUBLE SUBJECT (1 AND 2),
NOMINATIVE ABSOLUTE, PARTICIPIAL PHRASE

1. First, one teen-aged boy leaped from it.
2. Then two others leaped from it.
3. The last two were chasing the first toward the pool.
4. They were yelling loud threats.

ADVERB CLAUSE WITH DOUBLE VERB (1 AND 2),
PARALLEL ADVERBIAL CLAUSE, MAIN CLAUSE,
PARALLEL PARTICIPIAL PHRASES (5 AND 6).

1. The women on the lounges wakened.
2. They sat up abruptly.
3. The swimmers climbed from the pool.
4. The two teen-aged boys caught up with the first.
5. They threw themselves on him.
6. They bore him down to the grass.

MAIN CLAUSE, PARTICIPIAL PHRASE

1. One of the watchers screamed out.
2. She had caught the glint of a knife in the sun.

MAIN CLAUSE, ADVERBIAL CLAUSES PARALLELLED

1. The boy on the ground screamed, too.
2. The knife made its quick descent.
3. A horrible red gush spread over the front of his shirt.

MAIN CLAUSE, INFINITIVE PHRASE,
RELATIVE ADJECTIVE CLAUSE, ADJECTIVE PHRASE

1. The two boys moved quickly.
2. They picked up their victim.

3. He was lying there.
4. Now he was limp and still.

PARTICIPIAL PHRASE, MAIN CLAUSE
WITH DOUBLE VERB (2 AND 3), PARTICIPIAL PHRASE

1. They wasted no time.
2. They flung him into the back of their car.
3. They jumped in themselves.
4. They scratched off a minute later in a race for the gate.

PREPOSITIONAL PHRASE, MAIN CLAUSE,
RELATIVE ADJECTIVE CLAUSE

1. I was at my desk in the television station.
2. I had a phone call from the chief of detectives.
3. He wanted to know if I knew a certain boy.

ADVERBIAL CLAUSE, NOUN CLAUSE, MAIN CLAUSE,
PARTICIPIAL PHRASE, PARTICIPIAL PHRASE

1. I said yes.
2. He was a friend of my daughter.
3. He told me that a report had come in.
4. The report said the boy had been stabbed.
5. The boy was perhaps critically injured.

PARTICIPIAL PHRASE, MAIN CLAUSE, PARALLEL
NOUN CLAUSES AS APPOSITIVE (3 and 4)

1. I was shocked at first.
2. I suddenly remembered one fact.
3. This particular boy was famous for staging practical jokes.
4. This was probably one such joke.

NOUN CLAUSE, MAIN CLAUSE, ADVERB CLAUSE,
PARTICIPIAL PHRASE

1. This was true.
2. I discovered it later.
3. The boy was found.
4. He was washing red acryllic paint from his shirt.

NOTES

1. Earl B. Hunt, *Artificial Intelligence* (New York: Academic *Press,* 1975), p. 435.

2. Dennie Van Tassel, *Program Style, Design, Efficiency, Debugging, and Testing,* 2d ed. (Englewood Cliffs, N.J.: Prentice-Hall, Inc., 1978), p. 63.

3. Ernest Hemingway, "Cross country Snow," *In Our Time* (New York: Charles Scribner's Sons, 1925),p. 141.

4. Horace Newcomb, *TV: The Most Popular Art* (New York: Doubleday, 1974), p. 157.

7
GRACING
THE STRUCTURE

GOAL: To learn the devices for handling words in the revising process

"Euclid alone has looked on beauty bare," wrote Edna St. Vincent Millay of the Greek mathematician who founded geometry. Certainly, the order of structure imposed on some literary work may be one of its chief attractions. The beauty of a computer program—spoken of as its *elegance*—lies in the clarity with which it achieves complexity. For you and us, we continue to repeat, clarity is essential to the transfer of thought from one mind to another. Yet there are other aspects of writing to be considered in effective communication.

Now that we have discussed the paper, the paragraph, and the sentence, it is time to examine individual words—those thousands of small colored mosaics that we fit into sentences for action and image-making. Which do we select under certain circumstances? How do words achieve transition? What do they contribute to rhythm? What is diction? Metaphor? Such concerns will constitute the subjects of this chapter.

On the other hand, we might have labeled this chapter *Revising,* for most of the devices for gracing a paper are achieved in that critical stage.

REVISING

For some beginning writers, the actual writing of a paper or report is considered a two-step operation: (1) getting it all down on paper, somehow, and (2) recopying it to correct errors in mechanics, like punctuation and spelling.

Such people must find the program plan an absolute essential. Without such a guide, that second step must also include straightening out organization. No wonder the task seems so overwhelming!

But perhaps you have chosen a sort of in-between procedure. You started out with the program plan, but, as you progressed, you just simply *wrote* as ideas came into your mind.

In that case, you should remember that the algorithm can still be applied. If you make a practice of skipping lines in your original draft, you can easily adjust the internal organization of your paragraphs. Often a change in the subject of a sentence or switching one end of a sentence to the other will reveal the logic of your thought to your reader.

But what if you like to write, and you're determined to achieve a successful paper? Then revising may consist of several rewrites. Not everyone can anticipate the possibilities that a given statement may suggest. When a thought is down on paper—when it becomes tangible—it may offer additional avenues for exploration. And so the careful writer may rework a paper more times than the student with other commitments might believe.

For the person who genuinely enjoys the process of writing, the final draft is the most agreeable stage of preparing a paper. There is pleasure in refining thought: clarifying its continuation, smoothing out rhythm, polishing phrases and implanting just the right word in the right slot. For this person, revising a paper is akin to the satiny finish you apply to the bookcase you've just built, or the sugar glaze you drizzle over a lemony sponge cake.

To be wholly practical, the revision you do can make the difference between a reader's viewing your work as just another paper—or in perceiving it as a stand-out, well above average.

Transitions

We have not dealt with transitions thus far. Transitions simply transfer thought from one paragraph to another, or from one sentence to another. If in your short papers you were careful to follow the algorithm, and if you have limited the subjects of your sentences to the subject of the paragraph, you probably have not needed to supply extra directives. Now that you are writing full-length papers, however, you may unwittingly obscure your line of thought. Because of the additional length of your communication, you owe your reader this assurance to his understanding.

(Although transitions may vary, in most writing they consist of elements less than a sentence. We shall not classify them according to length.)

It is helpful to think of the thought that progresses through your paper as if it were water flowing through a pipeline. Your sentences are comparable to pipe connections that you fit together, taking care that no major leak occurs.

If your only guide to thought is the order in which it surfaces in your mind, then it may resemble the electric pulse in Enigma, the German coding machine.

That pulse bounces from key to key at random—around and around it goes, and where it ends, nobody knows!

Most people are aware of the need to supply transition between paragraphs. Such a link works best if it is provided at the beginning of the new paragraph, rather than at the end of the one you've just finished. Consider: You've just achieved that carefully designed development of thought—Do you want to blur its image in your reader's mind by introducing something new? How much better to do the opposite, to touch back to the previous thought in order to show that you've finished with it—and then to sweep into the new!

You have a dozen or more transitional phrases locked away in your word hoard; bring them out as you write, varying them rather than depending on one or two over and over. You remember what they are:

> moreover, however, therefore, first, next, finally, to begin with, on the other hand, similarly, in the second place, at the same time, in addition

There are many more. A minor rule says that if you begin a system of enumeration (first, second, third; to begin with, next, finally), you should be careful to carry it through. One suggestion: Do not use enumeration *within* your paragraphs. Keep it for the main points. Otherwise, you will confuse your reader, who, despite all your efforts, will never know where he is.

A simple and effective transition between two main points is to attach a subordinated reference to the former point in the new point's cover sentence. That is, wave goodby to the preceding thought, but keep the cover sentence's main clause—its subject and focus—on what is forthcoming.

> Although so-and-so (the preceding thought) is valid, we must consider (new thought).
>
> While this (preceding thought) takes precedence, it is clear that (new thought).
>
> Just as (preceding thought) suggests, the result was (new thought).
>
> Altering our perspective of (preceding thought), we come to see that (new thought).

Such a subordinate clause points out the finality of the previous thought, while the main clause announces your new concern.

We call such words and phrases or clauses *directional* signals. Fifty years ago, when traffic was a mere trickle compared to that today, the advance man for a circus drove into a new town ahead of the regular caravan, chalking big arrows on light poles and fences that indicated the turns to the town's circus lot. Your signals similarly prevent wrong turns into dead-end streets. Certainly they contribute to the good reception of your paper.

Here is an additional suggestion about the wording of the new cover sentence as it achieves transition from the former thought: Provide your reader with the general phrase *before* supplying the specific:

> *Not:*   Hobbies are a second point of difference between the twins.
>
> *But:*   A second point of difference between the twins is their hobbies.

Some writers automatically reverse the two ends, as though it were desirable to vary the wording of the main points. On a high level of writing this may be so; we are concerned, however, with communication. We *want* the reader to know that this is the new point; we don't want to confuse him, even for the fraction of a second it takes him to read to the end of the sentence. In the example about the twins, this advice matters little because of its brevity. In subjects of more depth, to throw out a fact before labeling it is to break your pipeline to his understanding.

As we saw in chapter seven, one way to cue the reader to the importance— or lack of importance—of a new fact is to subordinate it in your sentence. That is, you incorporate it in a clause or phrase that cannot stand alone, reserving what *is* important to the main clause, which can stand alone. Let us say that you've been writing about the economy of New Bedford. In the paragraph you've just completed you have discussed its reliance on whaling. Your junction of that paragraph (A) with the new paragraph (B) reads like this:

> *End of A:* Throughout the era of whaling, New Bedford stayed prosperous.
> *Start of B:* Petroleum was discovered in Pennsylvania in 1857, and this meant a new stage in New Bedford's history.

Better transition, that is, the linking of Pennsylvania's oil to New Bedford's whaling, is achieved by explanation and by grammatical subordination.

> *End of A:* Throughout the era of whaling, New Bedford remained prosperous.
> *Start of B:* When whale oil was replaced by petroleum, discovered in Pennsylvania in 1857, New Bedford entered a new and dismal stage in its history.

You should also supply transitional devices within the individual paragraphs of a paper. You achieve the simplest transition by the ordinary use of pronouns and the repetition of key nouns. It is helpful also to provide transitional words like *moreover, therefore, however, then, also, either* at the beginning of the sentence, or thereafter. Time and place should generally precede the statement in which they factor as development.

> Twenty years ago, Paul Taylor set off an explosion among aficionados of dance with a duet in which neither dancer moved for three minutes. In 1975, he again disrupted his world with the work that is now a classic— "Esplanade," a dance in which there is a constant motion, but not a single dance step. Today, his choreography seems to have progressed into the primitive world of primitive and dark tribal rites.

Answering the Reader's Expectancy

Revising is best achieved after a certain lapse of time that allows you to view the rough draft with critical appraisal. One of the weaknesses to check for is the sentence that leaves your reader's expectancy unfulfilled.

Thus, while some facts lie inert on the page, needing only to be absorbed, other sentences clearly signal the reader to expect certain information. Of this pair, what facts do you anticipate after the first statement?

> In most cases, the sacred rites are different for boys and girls. The Taulipang tribe practices scourging, hitting, or whipping. In the Pangwe tribe . . .

Here, the writer has omitted a step in the development of the algorithm. He needs to inform us how the rites differ; then he should let us know which unfortunates are scourged or whipped—boys or girls.

Consider this adjustment:

> In most cases, the sacred rites are different for boys and girls. Boys usually suffer more severe treatment. Among the Taulipang tribe, for example, the boys are scourged . . .

A little later, the same writer leaves the reader's anticipation unanswered:

> Most tribes have some kind of ceremonies leading up to the final rite. The Kung of the Kalahau desert have two or three stages of their puberty rite. Unlike many tribes, they do not force the ritual on any of their children.

After reading the second sentence above, the reader thinks, "Well, what are the stages?"

Better revision would have caught the following ambiguity, for the reader never learns whether the boy or the shaman kills the animal:

> After the dancing, a vertical line is cut in the middle of each participant's forehead and each boy is given a special "choma" haircut. The next step is the killing of a large animal. The boy is worn out by now; he has not eaten for more than a day.

This particular situation would have been avoided had the writer observed a cardinal rule: If a human performs an action, that human should be subject of the sentence. Desirably, the erring writer would have expressed himself like this:

> In the next step, the boy must kill a large animal. (A cow? Better to say a *dangerous* wild animal, or give specific examples.)

This weakness of using an abstraction as subject is often met in business writing, as we shall see in a later chapter. Here is an example:

> One fear of computerization is that it will create a high rate of unemployment. Repetitive clerical jobs, such as typing invoices in a typing pool or updating a ledger on manual cards, could interfere with security.

The reader eventually puzzles out the writer's intended meaning: those people now occupying clerical jobs may be replaced by a computer. Why didn't she just say so?

Later, this same woman relies on the indefinite pronoun *one*, remembering some long-ago lesson in objectivity.

> If one finds one's skills are no longer needed, changing skills and working to be indispensable is a good alternative. Close contact with the data processing people is a must ...

Consider the following version:

> If you are a clerical worker who fears that his skills will soon be no longer needed, you would do well to update your abilities and seek a new job, concentrating on ways to make yourself indispensable. You should maintain your contacts with data processing people ...

Face to face with the individuals whom she addresses, the writer of these impersonal sentences would never dream of being haughtily formal. In an effort to adhere to outmoded standards of correctness, however, she first ignores the reader, and then holds him at a distance.

Rhythm

Let's say that you are at a stage of revising an important paper or report. You set out to improve what you've written, crossing out a phrase here, adding explanations there. You work industriously all evening, convinced that this document will be your best writing ever.

The next day, you prepare to copy your masterpiece. To your horror, nothing reads right. Your sentences bump and jerk like trains in a freight yard. The mellifluous phrases that you so carefully shaped now seem at war with their neighbors. Even reading to yourself you hear clashing sounds.

You reach for your crying towel. To have worked so hard—and now to find the paper ruined! You can't even tell what's wrong.

The problem: Your revisions have destroyed the paper's rhythm. When you first wrote it, you were in a good writing mood and the sentences flowed smoothly. In your well-intended revisions, you took out words and phrases and replaced them without concern for the original rhythm.

You're not at fault. A good many people don't realize that prose has rhythm—not as marked as the rhythm of poetry, but a factor in good composition.

Just as some of us are not as good dancers as others, so some writers can dash off free-flowing sentences with no trouble at all. If you are not one of them, you can prepare yourself for good rhythmic writing without much trouble. Simply read for twenty or thirty minutes before you begin the actual writing process. Or listen to music—but be sure the beat is neither swift nor langorous, but somewhere in between. When you revise, test the sound of the sentence before you make replacements. Look for synonyms that have about the same number of syllables and stresses (or beats).

Put very simply, writing rhythms depend on the writer's emotion, use of punctuation, and choice of sounds and stresses. Have you ever dashed off an angry letter of protest? Chances are, its sentences were short and terse, in accord with your heartbeat and breathing.

> The new ruling is abhorrent to us! We will not tolerate such injustice! Rescind that abomination or you will know our wrath!

Those who are more placid by nature tend to write in long rhythms:

> She [Abigail Adams] was one of John's most reliable correspondents concerning the military moves of the Continental Army, and she also reported to him on the issues of the local government and the contemplated confederacy. She often tried to gain support for her husband by writing to her friends and emphasizing some point he had made, although she felt that her letters were written much too hastily and carelessly to be worthy of merit.

If you think of words as unbroken sound, then it is punctuation that breaks up this flow and thereby establishes rhythm. Commas, semicolons, periods, dashes— they all signal pauses of various duration, like the rests in musical notation. In revising, group your phrases so that punctuation breaks up the sentence at intervals. Long, limber sentences with no pauses render the reader—literally— short of breath. (Breath-portioned groups of words are also more easily comprehended.)

The use of word-sounds and stresses is a study all of its own. Your ear will tell you which sounds are harmonious together; don't forget to read your material aloud. The French novelist Flaubert, author of *Madame Bovary,* believed that a writer's words should be tested by reading in full voice. Every word of his masterpiece was declaimed to the grove of Croisset.

After your revision, head for the shower—not to sing, but to read aloud. The tile will bounce your words back to you, so that you hear your voice almost as you would hear someone else's.

(This is an excellent way to pick up repetitious phrases, or the use of *therefore* three times in four lines.)

THE IMPLICATIONS OF STYLE, TONE, AND DICTION

Beginning writers are often confused about the meaning of diction. Where does diction stop and tone or style begin?

You remember that it is always wise to define questionable terms. Here they are, differentiated:

> *Style:*   The acquired skills and techniques that characterize an individual's writing: typical sentence structure, favorite grammatical elements, personal rhythm.

Tone: (1) The attitude indicated by the writer toward his work and his readers. (2) The mood of the work itself and the devices employed to achieve that mood.

Diction: The selection and proper use of words. Good diction requires the suitability of the word to its context. Various levels of diction are defined: formal, informal, colloquial, slang.

Suppose we clarify these a bit.

Style is the result of our reinforced patterns of writing, such as the linking of main clauses that we mentioned earlier. A professional writer will develop a more complicated style that is based on his temperament, personal rhythms, educational level, and various other factors. To see extremes of style, you have only to read a page from one of Ernest Hemingway's short stories and then a page from William Faulkner's story "The Bear." Hemingway's bare, laconic sentences contrast markedly with the incantatory prose for which Faulkner is noted. Yet one writer is not necessarily rated higher than the other.

Probably it will not surprise you to learn that computer programmers develop a personal style comparable to that of writers more familiar to you. Like the differences between Hemingway's style and that of his imitators, the work of a professional programmer can easily be singled out from amateur versions of the same assignment.

(Incidentally, both the top-level programmer and the professional writer "see" in terms of images, as we'll demonstrate shortly.)

To indicate the artifice available to the programmer, we shall refer to an example cited by Thomas Whiteside in *Computer Capers*.

Two top-level programmers, specialists in penetrating computer security, were assigned to test an advanced computer-time-sharing system called Multics, supposedly so secure that the Pentagon could rely on it for storing highly classified defense information.

Even though they were allowed only the minimal access accorded every user, the experts soon ascertained that the computer's safeguards could be penetrated. In a short time they had written a program that would circumvent its supposed security checks, thus making Multics' data available.

We quote Whiteside:

> Essentially what they did, it appears, was to take advantage of the inability of [this] computer to make qualitative decisions. "We provided ways of making unexpected requests of the computer, and then looked to see how the computer responded to unexpected requests—things that would be nonsensical to a sensible user." [One programmer] said, "We watched to see how the computer might respond by itself doing something unexpected." In this way, they devised a method of entering from their terminal an informational request that the computer accepted as legitimate, and, proceeding from that, they wrung from the computer compliance with a sequence of other requests.[1]

Of course, this excerpt doesn't refer to the programmers' actual style of writing, as we've just defined style. Yet it strongly implies the individuality that would eventuate as style in writing, for style is very much a matter of skillful manipulation. You may believe us that style finds expression in algebraic notation as well as in other symbols—English words.

Tone is a matter of the writer's emotional attitude toward his topic. Thus, you might write angrily to a friend who failed to keep a prearranged date. Or you might pen a loving message to a small brother or sister. (In this situation, the simpler language you would use constitutes the letter's *diction.*) To a close friend, you might describe a humorous experience in dead-pan, naive expressions that will collapse your reader with laughter.

In student and much professional or managerial writing, tone varies little. That is, most often you represent yourself as a concerned, well-meaning, likable sort of individual. Almost always you will want to maintain this *persona,* for certainly it is the most productive.

And so we come to *diction,* a word that often appears in the margin of student essays. Basically, diction is suitability—the appropriateness with which you dress your topic for its purpose and its reader. If you wore tennis shoes to a formal White House reception, the other guests would blink—just as a teacher might raise an eyebrow to read, "Horatio was the guy in Hamlet who ..."

By college age, most people realize that the language we toss around in everyday life (estimated at 2,000 words) contains a number of expressions unsuited to the permanence of writing. Custom maintains that we don't—or shouldn't—write as we talk, even in fiction. A few minutes' consideration or a check with the dictionary is usually enough to clarify which expressions are unsuitable.

Levels of Formality

In your writing, either as a student or an executive, it is unlikely that you will need to know more than two levels of formality (unless your composition teacher believes in delving into the area of creative writing).

The first is that which you find throughout this book. Because we envision you, our reader, as a friendly person, sincerely committed to improving your skills, we suit our diction to that concept.

That is, our sentences employ first- and second-person pronouns (*we, us, you*). Occasionally, when we want to suggest something that someone other than you might do, we move into third person: *the student* (or *the reader*) must make *his* choice. (You remember that usage dictates the male pronoun; it becomes awkward and wordy to keep repeating *his or her*). We employ contractions freely, and very rarely we slip in an appropriate slang expression. If we can think of a good, short, image-making word, we prefer it by far to a many-syllabled Latinate term.

(If we must work with abstract nouns, then it becomes doubly essential to employ good action verbs.)

In summing up informal diction, we will point out its increasing popularity in information written for the general public. The Federal government has mandated its use in documents like insurance policies and other financial commitments that for so long clung to confusing legal terminology. Teachers have been brought in to assist bureaucrats to write on this more effective, understandable level. Only in law and other highly professional fields is the formal paper still encouraged. Probably that is why some college instructors continue to encourage it.

The great difference between the two levels is that informal diction results in subjective writing, with some reference to the human writer and reader on a person-to-person level, as we have said. Formal diction, on the other hand, represents objective discussion of the material. Most often, it omits reference to either writer or reader; if that becomes necessary, it continues to distance them bv the use of third person:

> The writer hopes that readers will overlook his omission of this area of the argument . . .

While contractions are banned, much of the subject-matter and terminology is abstract and perhaps particular to the writer's professional field.

A comparison of the two levels looks like this:

STYLE	HUMAN REFERENTS	SELECTION OF WORDS	CONTRACTIONS
Formal	the writer—he the reader—he	abstractions permitted, literary or professional allusions	unacceptable
Informal	I, we—you	concrete, image-making words familiar to college-level readers	acceptable

You need not be in doubt about which level of diction to employ. An instructor who requires a formal paper will certainly inform you of that fact (or you can ask). In business or a profession, some corporations make a handbook of instructions available to those of its executives who must write. General Electric publishes a full-length book entitled *Style Manual for Technical Writers,* as do a number of other great companies.

One thing more—Just as you are careful to wear clothes appropriate to a given occasion (a formal wedding, as opposed to a beachparty), so your choice of quotations and metaphor needs to match the level of your paper's diction. That is, you don't link something you read in a comic strip to a discussion of foreign policy. On the other hand, if you're presenting a plea for better safety for school children, you might well cite a comment from "Peanuts."

Just as we humans seem to hunger for order, for patterns, so we keep trying to reduce our concepts to what our senses can perceive. Like children who do not easily understand abstractions, our understanding craves concrete reality.

Highly creative people often "see" abstractions as images. The French philosopher Descartes formulated coordinate geometry while watching a fly buzz around the room. Suddenly, he writes, it came to him that the fly was doing algebra. Some medieval genius conceived the idea of representing Bible figures in a church's windows, so that illiterate people could see what until then they had only heard. Because the great satirist Jonathan Swift despised the falseness of courtiers who fawned and plotted for advancement, he depicts their Lilliputian counterparts engaged in degrading dog-like tricks and walking tightropes. Even mathematicians render meaning visible. Britian's George Boole represented a sentence's logic in algebraic notation; John Venn conceived of shapes that illustrated it. Today some top-level computer programmers evidently share that kind of vision. We quote from Thomas Whiteside's interview with one such talented individual—unfortunately a criminal who had milked several million dollars from his employers. He speaks:

> "In the work I do, I happen to visualize cost-accounting problems in geometrical or spatial metaphors. I tend to see figures in the shape of charts and graphs; I tend to see a cost progression as a curve with a certain shape and in a certain motion across a scale. When you see things that way, you don't need to burden yourself with a million details."[2]

All of these examples are intended to demonstrate the effectiveness of image-making words in writing. Not only are they invaluable in clarifying some concept, but they can add life and vigor and grace. Most often it is metaphors that effect this kind of magic.

You remember that one of the three ways to describe a thing or an action is to go beyond it and compare it to something else, as in analogy. Analogy generally describes an abstraction in terms of something familiar, usually an object perceived by the senses, an image. Metaphors are a kind of analogy, a briefer version.

Together with symbols and similes, metaphors are classed as figures of speech or *imagery*. You don't need to know which is which to enjoy their rewards, but here are simple examples:

metaphor	(an implied analogy)	He <u>wolfed</u> his food.
simile	(an expressed analogy using <u>like</u> or <u>as</u>)	He ate <u>like a wolf</u>.
		He snatched up great mouthfuls <u>as a wolf does</u>, obviously famished.
symbol	(A word that represents something more than its own meaning)	The peasants had directed all of their efforts to <u>keeping the wolf from the door</u>.

No doubt you have seen *wolf* in this kind of phrasing many times. It harks back to the distant centuries when wolves roamed Europe, driven by hunger to attack travellers and outlying peasant huts. As a metaphor it was old long before the Pilgrims reached this country. Therefore, the comparison of wolf to human eating is not a good metaphor. It has lost the elasticity that enables it to stretch from the thing being described to the thing that is the comparison. No electric pulse passes from one neuron's axon to the other's dendrite.

Any metaphor with which you are familiar is better avoided. It is likely to be old and tired if it just pops into your mind: off the beaten track, white as the driven snow, tired as a dog, pale as a ghost, innocent as a newborn babe, run like a rabbit, hot as fire. We use these and similar expressions thoughtlessly in speech. In writing, however, they do you no credit.

Our recommendation to employ metaphors, then, must also include the proviso that they be original and apt—that they fit—not like a glove—but like a high-priced wet-suit.

Vocabulary

Any style of writing requires a wide range of word choices. In informal writing, this does not mean a string of Latinate abstractions. Over and over authorities tell us that the simplest, clearest word is the best word. The student who "swallowed the dictionary" is not always the best writer in the class—or at least, not for that reason.

It is true, however, that the limited vocabulary of a good many students hampers their written expression or even their career. A young friend of ours, blocked from a desirable fellowship by a low verbal score on the Graduate Record Examination, took it again after memorizing most of a vocabulary text— and received the fellowship.

Next to a good dictionary, one of the most useful aids to word building is Roget's *Thesaurus*. While most other books of this kind are organized alphabetically, like dictionaries, Roget's is structured in sequences of closely related categories: similar, contrasting, and opposing concepts. At times when the right word continues to elude you, this design turns out to be considerably more helpful than alphabetized synonyms.

However, no thesaurus replaces a dictionary. All too often, student papers contain phrases so obviously inappropriate that the instructor recognizes their origin—from the thesaurus straight to the paper. All such words need to be checked against the more specific definition provided by the dictionary.

The criterion for the right word in the right place, then, is exactitude. If your word hoard is amply supplied with clear, picture-making words, no one will subject you to objurgation for refusing to obfuscate your meanings like this.

REAL-LIFE WRITING: TINA AND THE UNICORN

How does a writer make conscious decisions about improving a paper in the revising stage?

Let's follow diminutive Tina (whose mop of dark hair and deep tan suggest an Italian starlet) and see what she learns.

Tina works for the state in the Museum of History administration. Over in Historical Publications a vacancy in the staff of writers will be available next year—a job Tina would very much like to have. Although in college she had exempted freshman composition, to be sure of qualifying for the new job, she plans to take a late-afternoon refresher course at the University. As an advanced writing course, however, it requires a sample of prospective students' work as evidence of their ability. Remembering her childhood collection of unicorn figurines, she decides to write the history of the unicorn.

After unearthing a number of facts, Tina puts together the following paper:

THE UNICORN

Once famous from England to Islam to China, the unicorn has undergone some remarkable changes.

Our first introduction to this legendary beast is found in Greek and Roman classics, where, typically, it represented a mixture of several creatures. The ancients described it as having the head and body of a horse, the legs of an antelope, the tail of a lion, and a beard like a goat—with the single great horn of the narwhal.

To early Christians as well as to Jews and Moslems, the unicorn was the fierce creature mentioned in the Scriptures. Both Deuteronomy and Numbers tell of its great strength, and in Job it is said to "harrow" man. Probably for this reason, Scottish clansmen made it a "supporter" on the royal arms of Scotland. When the Scottish King James became James I of England, the unicorn was added to the lion on the royal English arms.

By the medieval period, the elusive beast possessed gentler, more romantic qualities. Although the courtly romances mentioned its ferocity, they maintained that it could be caught by a virgin, to whom it would go willingly. So popular was this belief that the Church, with its emphasis on symbolism, appropriated it. The unicorn was said to be Christ; the maiden his Church, and the fabulous horn (considered an aphrodisiac) became a means of purification. It would make poison harmless, or foul water clean. At royal courts, a cup carved from "unicorn" horn (probably rhinoceros) was used as a safeguard against regicide.

Today, the unicorn represents a fairytale creature famous for (obviously) its rarity. In its older significance, only literary works like *The Glass Menagerie* and "A Unicorn in the Garden" hint of its exciting past.

"Straight out of Dullsville!" Tina mutters to herself next day, re-reading it. Where was all the excitement, the magic? She has included the facts, but they seem so bare.

"I know it's not right—but what's wrong with it?" she wails later to her date, Court, who writes copy for an advertising agency. "It's grammatical; it has good sentence structure, and it reads well. Tell me what I should do to it!"

"Okay," says Court cautiously, "if you promise not to get uptight and defensive ..."

"Promise," Tina agrees, with a nod that sets her curls bouncing.

"Your first sentence—your cover sentence—suggests a surprise for the reader ... So build it up more; heighten the mystery. Stress the conflict between the expected and the real."

Tina writes busily in a small notebook.

"Do even more. *Show* us the unicorn as he looks now, and as he might have looked in action."

"Show; don't tell?" Tina suggests.

Court nods. "Remember, it's the single horn that distinguishes the unicorn from the bull or the stag ... Do more with that significance."

Tina continues to write.

"Quote the actual words of those references. They'll have far more weight than your just mentioning the fact that they exist."

"Will do ..." Her pen races over the page.

"Just two more comments. Provide more details; you must have found more than you give. Pack the rifts with ore, as Keats said."

"All right. What's the other thing?"

"Use good verbs."

"I thought I was using good verbs." She looks up in protest. "I cut out most of the *to be's* and *to have's,* except as auxiliaries."

"Yours don't suggest physical action. Get more movement into your sentences." He pauses to think, then gestures finality.

"Do all that, and you'll get off to a flying start." He puts his hand in his jacket pocket and brings out a small paper cylinder. "Hey—You told me your subject, so I brought you something."

Tina unrolls the paper. "A bumper sticker!" She reads and then laughs. "I BRAKE FOR UNICORNS. Say, is that a snide comment on that ticket I got?"

"Let's take a break from unicorns and go eat," says Court.

When Tina begins to rewrite, she makes a list of Court's comments that reads like this:

> Build a strong beginning to keep the reader reading.
> Stress the conflict: present vs. past, expected vs. real.
> Show, don't tell.
> Give extra stress to what's important. Don't just depend on the reader to pick it out.
> Give the actual words of quotations.
> Work in *action* verbs.

While she suspects that the paper could still benefit from improvement, time is short. As Tina hands in her essay, it reads thus:

THE MISTAKEN MYTH OF THE UNICORN

We see the gentle white unicorn so often these days, as small figurines in gift shops, illustrations for calendars, the subject of posters and book covers. Most people, associating the appealing creature with childhood's trusting innocence, would be surprised to learn its original symbolism, so much in contrast. The conversion of the ever-popular unicorn represents one of Time's great transformations.

The unicorn emerges from the mists of earliest history not as a shy, timid creature, but as raw generative force. He paws the ground with aroused male aggression, bugling his challenge, his superior strength powered by untamable arrogance that man seems to have envied. Across pages written in Arabic, Chinese, Sanskrit, and Greek he charges, head lowered to present the great narwhal's horn, eyes red-rimmed and vengeful, able to battle and best even an elephant.

"Canst thou bind him?" asks God of Job. "No, he'll harrow thee through the valleys." In Numbers 23:22, King James' translators wrote the marveling Hebrew words thus: "God brought them out of Egypt; he hath as it were the strength of the unicorn."

Such strength matched their own, no doubt thought the fierce clansmen in Scotland's bleak mountains. Thus, the Scottish royal arms display as "supporters" two unicorns rampant. And when their king ascended the English throne as James I, the unicorn joined the lion on the royal English arms, where it still remains.

But with the medieval interest in courtly romance, another aspect of the unicorn grew to importance. Noble ladies smiled when gallants described its male fierceness overcome by the power of love. Though men hunted it in vain, a beautiful maiden might bring it willingly to lay its head in her lap. Then hunters could kill it for its magical horn, an aphrodisiac.

So popular was this romantic tale that some Churchmen fastened on it a surprising reversal of meaning: The unicorn stood for Christ. As the fete-day for the fertility goddess Eostre became holy Easter, so the hunt was pronounced allegory; the unicorn's passion no longer bestial, but the Passion of Jesus; the maiden his Church; and the horn empowered, not for miracles of generation, but for those of purification. Even scholars believed that the horn could sweeten polluted water and render poison harmless. Until 1789 in France, the ritual of safeguarding the king's food with "unicorn" horn was included in the court ceremonial.

Today, however, both ferocity and miracles are lost in the fraying pages of time. What remains of the unicorn is only the bleached gilding of pleasant childhood illusion. Few of those who collect its pictures or figurines recognize the shade of its former power. Only in literature does an occasional faint challenge re-echo: in Tennessee Williams' *The Glass Menagerie,* for example, or in James Thurber's "The Unicorn in the Garden."

Although Tina's article runs somewhat long for what is basically a five-paragraph paper, its brevity does not warrant the research accorded a library or term paper. Because the library paper continues to be important in the academic world, our next chapter will present some possibilities of easing the strain it suggests.

SUMMARY

Many of the devices that improve the quality of writing are added in the revising stage. This is the time to arrange transition of thought both between and within paragraphs and to check sentences to see if they answer the reader's previously conceived expectations. In making changes, however, it is important to maintain the paper's natural rhythm. To check the smooth flow desired in good writing, reading aloud is an excellent practice.

Such writing rhythm is one aspect of a writer's individual style (or the pattern he comes to adopt), a style that is based also on his personal qualities and his tendency to favor certain structures and expressions. While variations in tone are a concern of the professional writer, in academic and managerial writing, suitable tone almost always reflects the writer as a concerned, friendly person who is knowledgeable about his subject. Diction, on the other hand, consists of the writer's choice between one of two possible levels: formal (objective) or informal (subjective). Formal diction addresses itself to the material, to the exclusion of possible readers. Informal diction implies more of the interaction of speech, relying more on image-making words and colorful allusions instead of polysyllabic expressions or professional jargon.

Because writing well on either level is a matter of the *exact* word, most people benefit from extending their vocabularies.

ASSIGNMENTS

1. Turn back to Tina's second paper and answer the following questions (e. requires a comparison of both papers).

GENERAL QUESTIONS
  a. What is the cover sentence? How many sentences are included in the introduction?
  b. The article has three main points. Which sentences express them?
  c. The link between the three subpoints of the first main point is not stressed. Can you determine it?
  d. Does Tina follow all of Court's suggestions? Find an example of each.
  e. Are the main points of both papers the same?

STRATEGIES OF DICTION AND STYLE
  a. Is the title of the second article an improvement on "The Unicorn," her first effort? What does it add?
  b. Why does Tina in her second paper omit any reference to the strange mixture of animals described in the classics, and to the rhinoceros as well? Did she have a valid reason?
  c. Do you find any cumulative sentences? What purpose do they serve? Read them aloud. Do they read smoothly?

   d. Find several sentences where Tina employs the device of reversal. Do you find a balanced sentence?
   e. Why does Tina capitalize Before and After? (Prepositions are not usually capitalized, even in titles.)
   f. Determine the varying kinds of transitions Tina uses between each pair of paragraphs.
   g. Do you find any references to the senses other than sight?
   h. In paragraph 3, Tina thought of substituting *trumpeting* for *bugling,* and, in the second sentence of the conclusion, replacing *faded* with *bleached*. What reasoning underlay her choices, do you think?

2. In each of the ten groups of short sentences below, first determine which is the most important. Then, retaining it as your main clause, subordinate the other sentences to it to form one good sentence. Utilize any forms you know: subordinate clauses, phrases, or single words.

   a. The day approached for our trip to West Point.
   b. The two girls began to pack.
   c. There was much discussion about the clothes they'd take.

   a. It was at a time in the Fifties.
   b. Girls wore small hoopskirts under their school dresses.
   c. Under their evening dresses they wore enormous hoops.
   d. These big hoops took up a great deal of space in a car.

   a. The girls' father grumbled.
   b. He could take only one suit himself, he said.
   c. The girls' clothes bags took up all the available space.
   d. The girls' bags obscured the view from all three back windows.

   a. We finally arrived at West Point.
   b. We checked into the Thayer Hotel.
   c. Most guests of cadets stayed at the Thayer Hotel.

   a. A porter carried in all the luggage.
   b. The girls' father expected him to complain.
   c. He had to make three trips.

   a. The porter laughed.
   b. He said that our luggage was only average.
   c. The most luggage brought by girls was in June Week, he said.
   d. That was when a number of marriages took place.
   e. June Week was graduation time.
   f. Cadets were not allowed to marry until graduation.

   a. Our youngest daughter had been invited by a plebe.
   b. A plebe is a first-year man.
   c. Plebes have almost no privileges.
   d. He could not come to meet us at the hotel.
   e. He could not even ride in our car.

a. Coty could not see him until the football game that afternoon.

b. It was the game between West Point and Penn State.

a. We knew where our plebe would be sitting in the stands.

b. He had sent us tickets close by his section.

a. We found our seats.

b. He saw us.

c. He waved to us.

d. It was a very inconspicuous wave.

e. Plebes are severely punished for showing affection.

3. As we mentioned earlier, Thomas Whiteside is a staff writer for *The New Yorker,* a periodical well known for a certain style and excellence. The two sentences that we reproduce below conclude his most interesting book *Computer Capers.* In order to appreciate his style, a matter of intricate structure based on parallelism and balance, we suggest that you study the sentences closely, answering the questions that follow the excerpt.

> Whether in the military, in government, or in business the designers of currently contemplated computer systems seem no more able to promise absolute solutions to problems of data security than chess players are able to foresee games in which White can never be beaten. And in the meantime, nobody knows what Trojan-horse programs may be lying in wait in computer systems until, at the appropriate signal, they spill out in acts of disruption and pillage, or what electronic dead souls may be flitting within the recesses of a system until, at the direction of some intent Tchitchikov at a keyboard terminal, they are mustered into ghostly but immensely exploitable legions.

a. Read the sentences aloud, noting their rhythm. Are you aware of the movement forward? Single out the verbs. Do they show action?

b. Find prepositional phrases of time and note their positioning.

c. Copy down each set of parallel or balanced elements, underlining those included in others. See how many you can find.

d. Note the comparison to see how Whiteside limits his subject-matter to computers, rather than going into some other area. He utilizes two literary allusions, one to the *Iliad* (Trojan-horse) and the other to Nikolai Gogol's novel *Dead Souls,* whose antihero is Tchitchikov. Note how he draws on them to enrich his material about computers, which can sometimes be dull reading.

e. Like dramatists, writers build images larger than life. The word *pillage,* for example, normally means raw violence of the most brutal sort, typical of conquerors in ancient times. The associations a word of that kind brings to the destruction of a computer are most effective. (One midwestern programmer grew so frustrated that he fired a round of shots into the machine, causing all the welfare checks in that city to be late.)

NOTES

1. Thomas Whiteside, *Computer Capers* (New York: The New American Library, 1978), p. 118.
2. Whiteside, pp. 94-95.

8
WRITING
THE PAPER
OR REPORT

GOAL: To achieve in-depth understanding of a subject by a grid of the templates, and from it to assemble a long paper, complete with formal outline

It is in the assembling of the library paper of several thousand words that the ready-made divisions of the template can be most appreciated. But what if a single template can't provide sufficient insight into a given subject? The logical solution, as we demonstrate in this chapter, is to combine them as a grid. Having done so, we provide a real-life situation in which such a paper is written, together with an overview of some conventions and a guide to the formal outline.

COMBINING THE TEMPLATES

Because each template concerns natural divisions that we make automatically, it is logical that, combined as a grid, they lead a writer into deeper understanding of his subject—or at least they open up avenues that lead to such discoveries.

The relatively new career of jury selection specialist works nicely with either template. We'll begin with the What-it-is triad (what it is, what it does, why it works) to acquaint you with this profession if you haven't read much about it.

One thing more: Although in criminal cases the prosecution sometimes retains a jury consultant, more often it is the defense who enlists his aid. We shall therefore word our statements as if that were the usual situation.

THE NEW SCIENCE
OF ENGINEERING JURY VOTES

WHAT IT IS

In both civil and criminal cases since the early 1970s, the skills of a new kind of consultant have made possible certain "wins" that in previous years might have been defeats. This highly trained consultant may be a sociologist, a social psychologist, or a specialist in market research. Whatever his academic training, his mission is to utilize scientific expertise to determine three kinds of information essential to the case: the possibilities of certain strategies, such as change of venue: the attitudes of the community toward certain relevant issues; and the best possible use of the attorney's hoarded peremptory challenges—the right to ban a juror without citing cause.

WHAT IT DOES

To obtain this vital information, the consultant busies himself long before the trial gets underway. Sometimes he checks the process by which the jury pool is drawn. He seeks out any imbalance that might permit a change of venue—for example, too many old people who might show prejudice against a young defendant. Usually, he sets up a survey that determines how members of the community react to controversial factors pertaining to the case. Such a survey makes clear the ideal juror, from the defense's point of view. It also furnishes information about attitudes essential to uncover during the *voir dire,* the questioning of prospects.

As the voir dire begins, the consultant takes his place beside the defense attorney. He watches eagle-eyed for the responses of each person to questions he has devised, questions that single out authoritarian types, broad-mindedness, prejudice, passivity. He scrutinizes tell-tale body language: Does the prospect avoid looking at the defense? Does he stiffen at certain areas of questioning? If he seems favorable, has he leadership qualities? This may be the best possible juror for the defense; in the jury-room he will round up other jurors to agree with him. Still, it is more critical to bar the wrong kind of juror, for a case is more easily damaged than upheld. For this reason, the consultant's skills are critical in the choice of peremptory challenges.

WHY IT WORKS

An offshoot of the new technology, the jury selection consultant walked into the courtroom hand-in-hand with the computer. Only a computer can process such large amounts of data at such speed. The decisions that earlier had been a matter of the attorney's experience now become large-scale statistics—the correlations between demographics and the community's state of mind. With the data from a thousand persons answering 100 questions each, the consultant can set up a weighted point system that assesses each prospective juror on a scale from 1 to 5. A Columbia University sociologist has said that such large-volume research can exercise up to 80% control over jury selection. That's a considerable increase from the attorney's 50-50 guess.

And now, let's examine the Divisions of Man development as a single paragraph, that emphasizes emotion, logic (practicality), and morality:

For the man or woman who enjoys a broad view of human nature, the career of jury consultant combines opportunities seldom matched in other fields. To begin with, the dramatic vistas it provides of behind-the-scenes crimes and corporate maneuvering are endlessly diverting. Each new case discloses fresh insights into human motivation, sometimes sordid and pathetic, sometimes greedy and power-driven. Moreover, such a career is highly paid. Specialists who have built a reputation of celebrated "wins" can easily command a thousand dollars a day. Fringe benefits incude travel expenses around the country, entertainment at leading eateries, large fees for making speeches at various conventions. Such remuneration makes possible the satisfaction that comes from a less publicized aspect of the consultant's career. Because of the large fees he receives in civil cases, he can and often does donate his skills to the poor and ignorant, especially in capital cases.

Thus, we have produced two short papers on jury selection as a career. Both are factual and accurate. Yet what if we wish to produce a longer essay than either of these? Or one that is less objective in tone?

What insights will be achieved if we form a grid of the two templates?

	WHAT IT IS	WHAT IT DOES	WHY (HOW) IT WORKS
EMOTION			
LOGIC (OR PRACTICALITY)			
CREDIBILITY (OR MORALITY)			

Essentially, exploring your subject like this achieves a deliberate screening of the objective through the subjective. But, you object, if that's what we want, why didn't we simply interpret the Divisions of Man in a more subjective light?

Had we done so, our exploration probably would have been too random, too aimless. When we create the grid, however, we are saying:

How is the *being* of this subject interpreted by human emotion? By practical reasoning? What affects the credibility of its *being?* Or its morality?

How is *what it does* (or *achieves*) seen in terms of emotion? In practical reasoning? How can *what it does* be made credible (or moral, or ethical?)

Can we think of *how* or *why it works* as emotional? As practical? Or logical? Does credibility have any significance here? Is there any spiritual factor?

Remember that Aristotle's quality of *ethos* may be interpreted (according to our needs) as either credibility or as moral or spiritual values. Like reputation and honor, they are two sides of the same coin. Credibility is accorded the individual by others, from outside in; moral values are inherent in the individual, reflected outward.

In working with the grid, you can expect only a certain number of answers to prove useful. We shall reproduce some of the possibilities in the subject of professional jury selection. Because it may be a controversial subject, we shall try to present something of a rebuttal.

First Level of Blocks

What jury selection is as emotion: By trial time, all individuals in the defense team (jury specialist, attorneys, the accused and his family) already experience an emotional link to each other. They are united by the belief that the odds are most often against a defense win and that they are the underdog. They expect prospective jurors to be subconsciously inclined to believe in the defendant's guilt (else why would he find himself in court?). Such telling details as the placement of the prosecution's table nearest the jury, they think, tend to weight the decision against them.

By this time, also, the jury specialist has come to know his client's background, with its (often) extenuating details. Such knowledge builds his emotional involvement. Even when his client is admittedly guilty, as a social science professional (in most cases), he views the individual with more than average sympathy.

The specialist may see the coming trial as high drama. In the voir dire that begins the trial, he plays the heady role of stage manager.

What jury selection achieves as emotion: The trial is highly competitive from the specialist's view. In the voir dire, he will try to induce an emotional rapport between his team and the eventual jury members as individuals.

Why (or how) jury selection works emotionally: Part of the jury specialist's judgment of a given prospect is based on his own emotional extension. He is well aware that the prospect's surface-level attitudes may not be consistent with his deeper responses. The jury will eventually find for or against the defendant, he believes, not as rational judgment, but for emotional reasons.

Second Level of Blocks

What jury selection is in terms of practicality. On any level, the selection of the jury is probably the most critical factor in the management of the trial.

For the client, it's an expensive means of narrowing the odds in his favor. The jury specialist he pays simply learns as many facts as possible about jurors and the community from which they come. He scales that information in such a way that he can evaluate individuals in terms of their probable attitude toward his client.

What jury selection achieves in practical terms: Before the trial, the specialist accumulates and evaluates information that may make possible a change of venue.

As the attorney questions prospective jurors, that information fans out as a wide range of possibilities that formerly were far too risky. With sufficient facts, he may be able to strike almost any prospect for cause, thus reserving his limited peremptory challenges for critical situations. He may accomplish certain strategies, like seating all passive jurors, who will forego taking any action. He may undertake to diffuse responsibility among the group. The selection process itself may become a means of delaying the final verdict for as long as possible.

Once the jury is seated, the specialist continues his fact-finding, directed now to specific individuals. His aids interview neighbors and business associates, check tax returns and directories. With this information, the attorney can "load" questions and avoid trouble spots. Even in his final appeal, he may beam certain references to specific jurors, twanging certain emotional chords suggested by the specialist.

Third Level of Blocks

What jury selection tactics are in terms of morality: They are a means to an end, a method of winning that is not always in the best interest of justice.

Why (or how) jury selection works for the specialist's credibility: As a package, the specialist is a highly skilled professional, gaining prestige from a record of wins much as does an attorney. The specialist testifies as an expert witness.

In addition to providing improved insight, the grid may suggest not only the main points of your long paper, but also the subdivisions that are necessary. Desirably, however, their headings should reflect your topic, not "Morality," "Practicality," "Emotion," etc.

Thus, it is entirely practical to think of such an assignment as consisting of three fairly short papers that can be constructed (and checked) separately at your convenience—a far less alarming prospect than starting at page 1 and writing through page 23. Instead of Mt. Everest, you need climb only three hills, none appreciably more difficult than the others. Then, as Odysseus says, you add Ossa to Olympus, and Pelion to Ossa. You simply bridge between the sections with sentences of transition, adding an overall introduction and conclusion.

SOME EARLY CONSIDERATIONS FOR THE LENGTHY PAPER OR REPORT

The paper or report generated by such a grid as that shown earlier usually requires considerable research, for most of us need to bolster our personal information with that gleaned from other sources. As you begin your research, it is helpful to be aware that both library papers and professional reports will generally fall into one of four classes: 1) They inform or show progress; 2) they analyze facts; 3) they maintain or argue a thesis; or 4) they persuade or recommend.

The first two are what we might term *to be* papers; they say that things are a certain way. As an example, suppose a beginning writer presents the possibilities by which public libraries can become computerized information centers. He collects various forecasts by authorities and rewrites them. If he also analyzes the facts, his paper will earn more credit.

The last two groups result in *to do* papers. Their writers support one side of a possible conflict or action. In effect, they say strongly, *Things should be done this way!* or, more gently, *Why not see it this way?* Because the writer conveys some emotional stake in his cause, these papers are likely to be more effective than the first two.

To continue our previous example: What if a taxpayer found out that in his community such an informational service was being planned by an out-of-town business concern for profit? The taxpayer might write a strong paper maintaining that the local library could handle such information without cost to the public. While the paper may be based on the same quoted authorities as the first, its potential is greater.

It is amusing to reach for a computer analogy. Computers are similarly of two kinds: digital or analog. Thus far we have referred to the digital type, an on-off, yes-no switching system that routinely implies, "Things are this way—or they're not." While the digital type works with separate units, the analog computer parallels a range of ongoing changes, such as lengths, voltages, or currents, as in the simulation of a plane's flight under varied conditions. This reminds us of the opinion paper, which reacts to its material with heated ardor or cool irony.

Of course, there are hybrid computers, just as there are hybrid papers that conclude straightforward facts with personal opinion!

Another way by which you can gain double value from your search is to keep in mind the requirements of the two templates (or a combination of the two).

If your topic is suited to a template, your selection of sources and facts need only consider those set divisions.

Even if your topic is inappropriate for these triads, watch for others that may prove useful as your paper's main points. You'll find that writers repeatedly lapse into patterns of triads (those who write about computers most of all). We selected these at random:

> For safety's sake, you should be concerned with the unseen by-products of VDT's: radiation, microwaves, and ultrasound.
>
> In five years, the average American can obtain extensive automated information services from commercial, private, and government sources.
>
> Twill is one of the basic weaves, the other two being the plain weave and the satin weave.

Other triads may be found in your sources, though perhaps less apparent. Throughout fiction you'll find that three examples prove the existence of some character's key trait. Or the rising action is comprised of three incidents before the story's climax. A character's downfall or trial often develops in three stages: bad, worse, worst. In famous stories, Edith Wharton and Chekhov provide wives with three husbands—serially, of course!

One further suggestion: Don't choose a topic simply because it offers an obvious triad of main points. No matter how efficiently you work, a library paper requires so much of your time and concern that it pays to look around for a subject you find interesting.

THE COMPUTER ANALOGY

The computer programmer also undertakes his task in separate modules, as you have seen earlier. In emphasizing this point, Dennie Van Tassel compares a long program to a business report (which, in turn, is similar to a library paper).

> Top-down program design is similar to top-down report writing. Reports are structured hierarchically and written from the top of the hierarchy. The design usually begins with ... a determination of the major tasks involved. ...

A little later he continues:

> A given task is broken up into a number of subtasks [that are] coded into a module with high reliability. This is the traditional and essential top-down approach used in building complex structures in other disciplines, such as engineering, mass production, and report writing. Each module can have one sentence describing the action that is to take place.[1]

To make clear divisions that will eventually become modules—large divisions of the overall program—is precisely what we urge for the library paper. All it takes is planning, and while not everyone has a flair for writing, everyone *can* plan.

(Think of how wearisome it is to copy and recopy a long paper because you haven't devoted adequate thought ahead of time!) As Van Tassel says, "[A]n hour of planning is usually worth five hours of programming."[2]

SOLVING THE PROBLEMS
OF QUOTING

Many writers worry less about planning, however, than they do about the problems of quoting. Once you have found all your material, how do you know what to quote, and how much? Obviously, if your knowledge of the tsunamu goes no further than its erroneous synonym "tidal wave," then every fact in your library paper comes from someone else. Yet you can't quote the whole thing! And then there are those troublesome footnotes—

As you recall, what we know comes to us from three sources: what we ourselves observe; what we learn from others (by conversation or reading or study), and what we derive from reasoning from facts gained previously. Most of the information that constantly laves our brain cells is learned from others.

Clearly, we can't begin to give credit where credit is due, except in the most specific situations. It is those specific cases that you will need to footnote. The rest is termed general information. It can be illustrated by the facts you found in the paragraphs about President Kennedy. Such items appeared in headlines in virtually every paper in the country. They form the bulk of facts that an informed person living in that era would remember.

But suppose we were to write scandal, attacking Kennedy's morality, or questioning his patriotism during his service in the Navy. To make such statements, obviously, we must cite authorities and footnote our sources. In so doing, we would illustrate two of the three reasons for quoting: We achieve credibility for our dubious statements, and we recognize the efforts of the original author, the long months he may have spent in researching the information. The third reason applies to the original writer's choice of phrasing. You give credit for a felicitous expression you borrow—the phrase that provides just the right words in the right place. Thus, writers of the Sixties continued to quote a dramatic statement from the speech in which Kennedy accepted the presidential nomination, July 20, 1960. In it, he seemed to foresee the changes the decade would introduce.

> We stand today on the edge of a new frontier—the frontier of the 1960's—a frontier of unknown opportunities and perils—a frontier of unfulfilled hopes and threats.

Scholarship sees itself—and, by extension, education—as a last bastion of integrity. When you write a paper for a college class, it is considered a scholarly paper. As an educated person, you are able to build on the ideas of others while giving them credit.

Paraphrasing

Obviously, it isn't possible—or desirable—to quote great indigestible hunks of material from professional authors. People who are not aware of this are likely to write what is called "a scissors-and-paste paper," a paper in which there appear almost as many quoted words as those the writer originated. A teacher may not accept such a paper for credit; the purpose of an assignment is to elicit the student's own ideas and phrasing.

The way to avoid such an over-supply of quotations is to paraphrase. You read the material carefully for basic comprehension, and then, laying it aside, reword what you have read.

Often, you may need to condense the material you are paraphrasing, to present its meaning in fewer words. If the material is well written, it is probably constructed (like the program plan) with topic sentences and main supports. In that case, it is helpful to copy those key sentences and then restate their facts in your own words.

The information below that we use as an example of paraphrasing serves also as background for the article at the end of this chapter.

> Without doubt, "caste" originated in the economical division of labor. The talented and most intelligent portion of the Aryan Hindus became, as was natural, the governing body of the entire race. They, in their wisdom, saw the necessity of dividing society, and subsequently set each portion apart to undertake certain duties which might promote the welfare of the nation. The priesthood (Brahman caste) were appointed to be the spiritual governors over all, and were the recognized head of society. The vigorous, warlike portion of the people (Kshatriya, or warrior caste) was to defend the country, and suppress crime and injustice by means of physical strength; assisted by the priesthood, they were to be the temporary governors in the administration of justice. The business-loving tradesmen and artisans (Vaisya, or trader caste) had also an important position assigned under the preceding classes or castes. The fourth, or servile class (Shudra caste) was made up of all those not included in the preceding three castes. In ancient times, persons were assigned to each of the four castes according to their individual capacity and merit, independent of the accident of birth.[3]

PARAPHRASE

> In India, the rigid hierarchial divisions of caste probably began as apportioned responsibility for the nation's welfare by the Aryan Hindus, an enlightened ethnic group. In their era, social, economic, and political authority was assigned by merit, rather than by birth. Pre-eminent were the Brahmans, entrusted with social and religious guidance. Next below them were members of the warrior caste, charged with the nation's defense and its adjudication. Third in rank was the caste of merchants and artisans, while in last place was a servant case that encompassed all those not otherwise designated.

The two requisites for paraphrasing are simply (1) an understanding of the material, and (2) a reasonably good vocabulary. For these reasons, the student might find it difficult to paraphrase material about optic fibers; he has no real margin of information about the subject and no terminology beyond that supplied by the author.

Footnoting

While footnotes may be used by a writer to comment on his material or to direct the reader to other material, it is well to hold such extra messages to a bare minimum. An excess number of footnotes is distracting; unless you have a captive reader, he is likely to ignore footnotes altogether or to stop reading the paper. Provided you paraphrase sufficiently, you should have no more than three or four footnotes per page. There are exceptions, of course.

Footnote forms vary according to discipline (that is, for an English essay or an engineering report) and a given teacher's or employer's preference. If some special form is required of you, you will no doubt be informed of the requirements and where examples are available.

Rather than present half a dozen pages of varying possibilities, we simply provide an overview of footnoting and bibliography forms that are most often needed. Additional examples are available in the sati essay that follows. Rarer forms may be found in any good handbook. (All forms should be double-spaced.)

Identifying Sources

FOOTNOTES

The source of every quotation should be identified in one of three ways:

In a footnote at the bottom of the page
In an endnote, on a separate page that precedes the bibliography
As a page reference in parenthesis, directly following the quotation (An explanatory first footnote should provide the usual information.)

BOOK'S FIRST FOOTNOTE (NOTE FIVE-SPACE INDENTATION.)

Author's name in regular order, book's title, (City: Publisher, year), page no.

Ex: [1]Jane Walpole, *A Writer's Guide* (Englewood Cliffs, N.J.: Prentice-Hall, 1980), p. 32.

ESSAY FROM BOOK

Author's name in regular order, essay's title, book's title, editor's name (City: Publisher, year), page no.

Ex: [1]R. P. Blackmur, "Emily Dickinson's Notation," in *Emily Dickinson: A Collection of Critical Essays,* ed. Richard B. Sewall (Englewood Cliffs, N.J.: Prentice-Hall, 1963), p. 82.

MAGAZINE'S FIRST FOOTNOTE

Author's name, article's title, magazine title, issue date, page no.

Ex: ¹Wolf Von Eckhardt, "A Pied Piper of Hobbit Land," *Time,* August *23, 1982, p. 62.*

SUCCESSIVE FOOTNOTES

Author's last name, page no. (If citing two books by the same author, provide key word from title.)

Ex: ²Blackmur, p. 82.
³Von Eckhardt, "Pied Piper," p. 62.
⁴Von Eckhardt, "Architecture," p. 14.

Except for the parenthesis and colon of the book's publishing data, footnotes require commas.

BIBLIOGRAPHY

It is now customary to cite in your bibliography only those works from which you actually quote. Bibliographical references provide the author's name reversed, and all lines but the first are recessed to facilitate finding one reference.

BOOK

Author's name, last name first. Book's title. City of Publication: Publisher, year.

Ex: Walpole, Name. *A Writer's Guide.* Englewood Cliffs, N.J.:Prentice-Hall, 1980.

ESSAY IN BOOK

Author's name, last name first, Article's title. Book's title. Editor's name in regular order. City of Publication: Publisher, date.

Ex: Blackmur, R. P. "Emily Dickinson's Notation." In *Emily Dickinson: A Collection of Critical Essays.* Ed. Richard B. Sewell. Englewood Cliffs, N.J.: Prentice-Hall, 1980.

MAGAZINE

Author's name, last name first. Article's title. Magazine title. Issue date.

Ex: Von Eckhardt, Wolf. "A Pied Piper of Hobbit Land." *Time.* August 23, 1982.

As opposed to the footnote's use of commas, the facts of the bibliographical references are separated by periods. The bibliography comes last in the set of essay pages.

The foibles of footnoting and bibliography are concerned with three blocks of information: writer(s), title(s) of publication(s), and publishing information (again three: city, publisher, date).

CHANGING TREE TO OUTLINE

Next to the idiosyncracies of quoting, students seem not to remember the conventions of the formal outline. Because such outlines are essential factors in both academic and professional reports, we'll move from the comfortable structure tree into the formality of the traditional outline.

In place of the open-ended tree that allows for new branches and twigs at any stage, the formal outline is much like a list. Once it assumes its final form, there is no easy way to make additions that maintain the pattern of subordination. Thus, a good many students do not bother with showing such relationships until the paper is completed. If more people did their planning with a structure tree, perhaps they would encounter less difficulty with organization.

Admittedly, for the reader of the paper the outline is less trouble to follow because of its compactness. The bones of quite a long paper will fit on one page, available at a glance. (For this reason, sentence outlines are less practical than phrase outlines.) Since you should understand the outline as well as the structure tree, we shall present the organization of the sati paper in both forms.

You will have no trouble with the outlne if you remember two basic factors: the top-down order of the notation and the old rule that the whole is the sum of its parts.

> Numbers alternate with letters; numbers first. The uppercase symbol precedes the lower case. Indentations represent the descending levels of the hierarchy.

That information translates into a representation of our algorithm:

    I.

      A.

        1.

          a.

The Roman numerals precede the Arabic; the scholars who laid down these rules idealized Latin. The capital letter precedes the small letter.

Remember to indent clearly, for the indentations indicate descending levels of importance.

I. One of the three main divisions of the paper.
  A. A main support of that division
    1. A minor support
      a. Further explanation or illustration.

Now for that ancient concept of the whole as the sum of its parts. Suppose we think of the body of a paper as represented by a circle, a pie that is progressively

126

divided. First, you section it into its large divisions or modules: I, II, III. Then you begin on the first division and separate it into the number of subdivisions suggested by the kind and amount of information available: A, B, C. Again you section, starting with A; its subdivisions are Arabic numbers. Their parts, in turn, are lower-case letters. You return to the second large division, II, and follow it down in similar fashion; finally, you do the same for III.

(This is exactly the order Marian Bohl suggested for the planning of a program, as represented by the tree diagram.)

The idea behind all of these divisions is that the parts could conceivably be reunited as a whole. The circle includes no more and no less after the operation than before. You can see how the indentations imply that the minor points add up to their heading:

A. FBI training
   1. In the classroom
   2. In the field

B. FBI supervision
   1. Of the public
   2. Of its own employees

C. FBI values
   1. As it sees itself
   2. As others see it

To bear out this concept of unity, it is desirable to structure elements under a given heading in the same grammatical form (here, as noun phrases and prepositional phrases).

We mention the pie for the reason that it bears out the need for a certain relationship that is otherwise difficult to explain. That is, all the slices must remain one kind of pie. If put back together, one section cannot be lemon, another chocolate, and the third blueberry. You should feel the same kind of rightness about your divisions as is evident in the templates: body, mind, and spirit—not body, mind, and ability to play chess.

Why isn't the thesis part of the pie? Because the thesis represents the whole pie. It is the sum of all those divisions, another version of the whole.

Turn now to the structure tree and outline that precede the sati essay to note how the nodes of the first are represented by indentations on the outline. After you have read the essay, examine the two more carefully in light of your additional information.

SELECTING A TITLE

For the professional writer, a title is a matter of considerable thought. In literary work, the title may be a key to the underlying meaning, deliberately obscure. In fiction, it is much more than meagre identification; it is a brief sales message: Read me! Writers often line an innocent title with the brass of irony. The reader's discovery of the loaded meaning heightens both his pleasure in reading and his respect for the writer.

Irony seemed particulary appropriate for the sati essay. Shannon, its writer, thought immediately of a well-known play by Christopher Fry, *The Lady's Not for Burning* (1948). In its medieval setting, a professional soldier, weary of life, saves a girl from being burned as a witch. Shannon's irony lies in the fact that, while Fry's play celebrates life, sati celebrated fiery death.

REAL-LIFE WRITING
SHANNON AND SATI

A year ago, lively, dark-haired Shannon enjoyed a pleasant suburban life as a wife of a young, well-established executive and mother of three preschool children. Now she finds herself at a remote university campus where her husband has become an undergraduate again, his first step into a new life and a new profession. This drastic change in income, status, and locale, Shannon finds, requires adjustment for the wives of other students similarly placed. The college accordingly maintains a weekly counseling session where their problems are discussed.

After the most recent meeting, she comes in frowning.

"I have to write a paper on suttee," she tells her blond, lanky husband Chad. "Only it's spelled s-a-t-i."

"Suttee?" Chad lays down the Greek text he's studying. Tiredly he rubs the furrow between his eyes. "Suttee? That's a strange subject. Is everybody writing on the same topic?"

"No." Shannon begins to pick up the toys strewn around the room. "Blanche has to write on that Chinese custom of binding women's feet. And somebody else is doing hetaerae, whatever that is. Mr. Gaskill wouldn't explain. Mildred's got Eskimo home life. Peggy drew the Oswal community in Mewar." She makes a face. "I guess he's just sending our minds around the world—while we're stuck up here on this mountaintop."

A strange expression crosses Chad's face. Shannon's chin juts forward. "What are you smiling about?"

"I think he's got something else in mind."

"What?"

"Wait and see . . ."

The next afternoon Chad comes in with a big armload of books. "You can use these for your paper," he explains, dropping them on the couch beside her.

Shannon looks through them. *"India: An Anthropological Perspective,"* she reads. *"The Position of Women in Hindu Civilization*—Hey, look! This was published in Delhi! 50 Rupees. *Indian Women* . . . So was this one. *Within the*

Purdah—This one's over a hundred years old! Look at this picture of a little girl and her adult husband ..."

After a few minutes, she leans forward, a worried expression on her face. "I don't know a thing about sati. Won't I be plagiarizing practically every sentence I write? And how will I know what to quote?"

"Look at it this way ... Your paper will contain three classes of facts." He begins to tick them off on his fingers. "First come those that are general knowlege—like, say, the Hindu Holy Trinity."

Shannon's dark eyebrows ask a question.

"Okay, so most Americans don't know that. But it's an unarguable fact. You'll find it in an ordinary dictionary or an encyclopedia. So that's general knowledge. The second kind of fact is really opinion—something debatable. A few people believe it; most don't."

Shannon nods. "Like Columbus believing the world was round."

"Right. "You'll probably link opinion with the third kind of fact: what needs to be proved. Some statement or statistics that your reader would doubt, unless he sees it there in quotation marks."

"I get the idea."

"When you start your reading, you'll soon recognize the differences between the three classes of facts." Chad smiles encouragement. "Those that all the authors present are general. But suppose you read that 100 women were sacrificed at one time. That needs proof."

"A hundred?" Her face mirrors disbelief. "Why would they do it?" Then she glances at the pile of books. "How will I know what notes to take, if I don't know what points I'll be making? I can't bear to think of writing down a lot of stuff I won't use in the paper."

Chad goes to his desk and begins to rummage through its pigeonholes. "That's where the use of a template saves a great deal of time. A template gives you ready-made divisions. Whenever you come across facts that seem appropriate to a given division, you note it on a card." He drops a pack of notecards in her lap. "In the right-hand top corner, just write the division of the template. On the left, the author's last name and the page. Then put the fact into your own words on the card. If the fact seems like something you'll have to prove, copy it accurately and put it in quotes. Use a different card for each fact and each quote. That makes it easier to subclassify the material that supports each main point."

"That's clear enough," Shannon agrees. "Okay. So what's a template?"

Chad begins to explain, citing simple examples of the two templates. Then he draws a grid and shows her its possibilities for increasing her perception of a subject.

"Now you can classify the information that you read as you go along," he finishes.

Shannon begins to read. Soon she is so fascinated that she is writing card after card, commenting aloud at intervals.

"Did you know that the word for *widow* also means *harlot?*" she asks. "People still think widows bring bad luck!"

"Honey, that's the fourth time you've interrupted me."

Thereafter she reads in silence, her face registering various degrees of indignation and horror. That night, the last words she says before going to sleep reflect the unanswered question. "Chad, why would widows consent to being burned alive? Why would their families let them?—Make them, sometimes! Why?"

In three nights she has gone through all the books. While Chad studies, she sorts out her thick sheaf of notecards according to the divisions of the template. The information for the *what it is* division is right there before her in a fan of cards. "This is just great!" she murmurs.

With no trouble at all she forms a structure tree for the first division. "Why, I can do the actual writing one division at a time! Then fit the three together!"

The thought of avoiding the problems she'd had in college with long papers is cheering. After she works up the rough drafts, she can simply unite them under one cover sentence and then supply transitions between them. After that, she'll tackle the introduction. She remembers that it's a good idea to leave that until last.

The night the reports are due, Chad waits for Shannon to come home. She marches in with a glint in her dark eyes.

"So—How did your paper go?" he asks cautiously.

Shannon grins. "It went fine." She kicks off her shoes and plumps down on the couch. "We wives learned a lot. We can be beautiful without having our feet bound. We don't have to send our husbands off to courtesans. We don't have to chew leather for our husband's boots. And we don't have to grow up in our in-laws' house."

She slings a cushion at him. "We may get burned up with our husbands now—but it's only temporary!"

OUTLINE

    I. (thesis) Because the high road to sati was shored up by the self-interest of others, wives both willing and unwilling lay down upon the pyre.
   II. (body) The needs it served
      A. In its bonding of myth and custom
        1. Its origins
        2. Its growing popularity
        3. Its variations
      B. In its negative reinforcement for the woman
        1. Her loss of purpose in life
        2. Her assets as liabilities
        3. Her essence reversed
      C. In its positive reinforcement
        1. For the wife: ingrained ideals
          a. Of familial obligation
          b. Of disdain for pain
          c. In the tenets of religion

    2. For relatives
       a. Achievement of prestige
       b. Increase of inheritance
       c. End to family friction
    3. For the clan
       a. Requirements of men
       b. Requirements of women
       c. Control of leaders
III. (Conclusion) Sati as the safeguard to status; compulsion as evidenced by wholesale sacrifices.

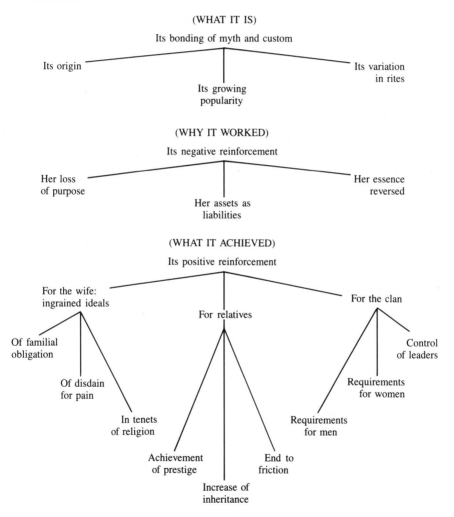

THE LADIES FOR THE BURNING

    The widow's choice to die in flames beside her husband's body—for twelve centuries that was the persisting ideal of the Hindu rite of sati. For the high-born woman, sati climaxed a pre-puberty marriage to which she had been led at eight or nine, trained for a single role—to serve and reverence her husband as a god. If she suffered the dismal fate of early widowhood, society saw that as punishment for some pre-existing sin; its paramount concern became her probable misbehavior, and thus it was better that she die. Until at least 1960,[1] wives both willing and unwilling perished on their husband's funeral pyre, for reasons Westerners have trouble comprehending.

WHAT IT IS (DEF'N)

The word sati represents the bonding of myth and custom. Sati, Sanskrit for virtuous woman, was the name assigned the consort of the god Shiva, who took her life when her father showed disrepect to her husband. As an honorable designation, "virtuous woman" came to be applied to the wife who consented to join her husband in death, no doubt a holdover of the widespread preliterate practice of providing comforts for the dead.

While sati occurred sporadically at first, as an obligation it began to build with the first Moslem invasion in the sixth century A.D. Gathering force like some great juggernaut, its popularity increased until the British outlawed it in 1829. In the sagas of the warrior castes, eulogies celebrated the courage of proud queens and great leaders' wives who matched their husband's bravery in the face of death. For other reasons, too, the custom spread; instead of lessening as western culture moved into India, it actually reached its peak as the British took command. British official figures for the 1815–1828 period account for 5,099 satis in the Calcutta Division, where it was most often practiced.[2]

In interpretation, the rite of sati implied slight variations in actual practice, depending on the geographical areas, and, apparently, the stoicism of past widows. In the ritual most admired, the widow was taken in a grand procession to the cremation grounds, where she donned all her insignia of married bliss (as decreed by the sacred writings), together with the symbols of her womanliness: mirror, comb, and betel leaves. Finally, she bid farewell to her relatives. Then, ascending the funeral pyre, she placed her dead husband's head in her lap and waited for the flames.

In sections where the widow's dedication might be in question, precautions were taken against her last-minute change of heart. To avoid that disgrace to the family, widows "were often drugged or plied with liquor and made virtually senseless."[3] In some areas, the funeral pyre was piled in a deep pit, into which the widow jumped or was pushed. In Uttar Pradesh and Gujarat, she was shut up in a tiny hut built for the occasion. In other areas, her feet were bound to poles, or relatives held green bamboo across her body, lest she should lose her courage.

While all authorities agree that unwilling victims were sacrificed, enough widows chose to endure the agony to raise the obvious question: What pressures continued the practice into modern times?

WHY IT WORKED

For the widow, the ordeal of sati received strong negative reinforcement. The miseries of widowhood invariably figure in every discussion of Hindu domestic life. Quite simply, everyone agreed that her purpose in life had ended, since she was forbidden to remarry. Overnight she lost whatever consideration her wifehood had afforded. Speaking of widows in contemporary times, anthropologist Stephen A. Tyler writes, "So low is her status that one of the worst curse words in Teluga is vedava (widow)."[4] In return for minimal economic support, she must drudge in her in-laws' house, barred from any family socializing, restricted to the innermost rooms. If she has not borne a son—the duty both religion and society demanded—then her miseries are redoubled. Unable to read and write (writing might lead to "correspondence with forbidden friends and paramours"[5]), lacking any skills except for wifehood, the widow is condemned to a future devoid of mitigating pleasures. Existence offers only continuing mistreatment.

(CONTRAST)

In the days of sati, perhaps an even greater adjustment was that of finding her feminine assets suddenly deemed liabilities. As a wife, her physical beauty had increased her value to her husband. She had been taught to enhance it, to maintain the abundance and sheen of her hair, to coif it in intricate styles. She had learned to move gracefully, to adorn herself with tinkling ornaments and musky perfumes. As a widow, all such feminine embellishments were denied her. Her head was shaved; her marriage bangles broken on her wrists and ankles. Her bright silken saris were replaced with harsh white cloth.

After the pre-puberty marriage, her sensuality had been encouraged and developed, according to the view that "women were more libidinous than men."[6] In the Rigveda, one of the most sacred authorities that governed Hindu thought, a husband expresses "his exuberant appreciation of [his young bride's] amorous skill."[7] As a widow, her arts rendered her dangerous to the family. The more successful had been her charms (as indicated by her husband's preference for her), the more zealously she would now be watched. "She was seen as "a potential source of sexual license," Tyler tells us, "her pent-up sexuality" a threat to the honor of three families: her husband's, that of any children they might have had, and that of her own people."[8] The Ramayana warns, "The very greatest danger that can overcome a woman is widowhood."[9] In one dialect, the word for widow is synonymous with harlot.

Not just her femininity, but the very essence of her womanhood was considered to have changed. Hindu thought imbues womankind with two opposing qualities, the beneficent and the malevolent, fertility and death. As mother, she represents the best qualities associated with her sex: warmth, sustaining love, devoted service. In a household dominated by her mother-in-law, her motherhood is the one achievement that accords her some respect. As her son grows, she in turn will be revered.

As a widow, however, she is seen as a vessel filled with evil spirits. Like the fearsome Kali garlanded with skulls, the widow arouses superstitious fears of disease and death. Whatever goes wrong in the house that harbors her is laid at her door.

> Traditionally, even the sight of a widow was inauspicious, and before setting off on any important business, men would call out, warning all widows to stay out of sight.[10]

No wonder that some widows saw immolation with its brief anguish and eternal triumph as less harsh than the reality of widowhood.

WHAT IT DOES (ACHIEVES)

While widowhood could and did overwhelm a woman in blackest misery, the innate life force in most people shudders back from agonizing suicide. What positive rewards led a healthy young woman to answer yes to self-immolation? What induced the families to concur? What was the climate of the community, its public opinion? With the widow as the core of successive widening circles, sati seems to have been the response to a number of tragically human motivations.

(CAUSE AND EFFECT)

Having been raised after the age of 8 or 9 by her mother-in-law, the widow was clearly conditioned by ideals instilled in her from childhood. Her act upheld familial obligation, disdain for pain, the tenets of religious authority. Those were the standards of the high-caste Hindu, to whom the maintenance of status was essential. Noblesse oblige! In Kipling's poem about British efforts to prevent sati, the newly widowed Queen rallies other wives and concubines thus:

> The Boondi Queen beneath us cried:
> "See now that we die as our mothers died
> "In the bridal-bed by our master's side!
> "Out, women! To the fire!"
>
> "The Last Suttee"

Moreover, such an ordeal, while incredibly horrible to contemplate, must have been mercifully quick. The pyre was instantly combustible, the blaze fierce and hot. (Western societies might remember the slow fires by which they burned witches.) Breathing in the intense flames, the victim's lungs must have been immediately seared.

Like family honor and proud disdain for physical pain, the tenets of religion were all-important to girls of the warrior caste. In the years following the first Moslem invasion, religious authorities recommended sati, as the older scribes had not. Instead of husband and wife being separated after death, they wrote, the wife's sati would enable them to be gloriously united for eternity. Her unselfish act would purify the husband of his most grievous sins. Even if she, too, had led a dissolute life, her sati would cleanse them both. A passage from the Parasarasmriti is often quoted:

> [J]ust as a snake-charmer forcibly drags out a snake from its hole by force, so the Sati takes out her husband from hell and enjoys heaven with him for three and a half crores of years.[11]

To become a Sati, then, was the ultimate service a wife could render the man she had been trained to worship. In that light, the persuasive force that conveyed sati through the centuries to the present is best illustrated by personal testimonial, the sati of Professor A. S. Altekar's sister. On 17-1-1946 (sic.), he writes, Mrs. Indirabai Madhav Udgaonker "committed herself to flames within 24 hours of her husband's death, in spite of the pressing entreaties of all her relations" and "the presence of a sucking child."[12]

Relatives who not only encouraged the act of sati but even forced it on the widow responded to motivations apparently less noble. Having been initiated by noblewomen, sati by a terrible irony spread to families seeking prestige. By 1800, weavers, barbers, masons, and other tradesmen had begun to pressure widows to become satis, as shown by the sati stones that commemorate their courage.

Moreover, after widows could inherit property (although it was managed by a male relative), the death of a legatee resulted in larger shares for the others.

An additional factor also weighted the situation, as suggested by the earlier reference to jealousy among the women of the household. The death of the widow removed her as a cause of domestic friction and dissension, a troublemaker among sequestered women who bickered and jockeyed for power. And she was, of course, inauspicious, often being blamed for whatever misfortune caused her husband's death.

While such a complex set of reasons obviously operates forcefully on the individual families, the contemporary reader with some knowledge of social psychology feels that such reasons are insufficient for sati's longevity. Other cultures have rested family honor in women's chastity without such dire results. Why, in a relatively late period of history, was sati deliberately woven into the fabric of religious observance?[13]

While the answer is obvious to Indians and those who know India, the contemporary reader requires some study to uncover the implications of <u>family disgrace</u>. It then appears that those fourteen centuries of lauded sati rest on a tripod of facts, true or believed true.

1. The caste system, post-dating the Vedic period, ranks classes of people according "to inherent degrees of purity and pollution" (from Latin castus, pure, chaste).[14] A person is permanently polluted by virtue of his <u>birth</u> in one of the four basic castes.

2. The sexual union of a high-caste woman with a man of lower caste (in marriage or not) not only defiles her and her family beyond purification, but contaminates <u>the entire clan</u>, diminishing its status in the eyes of the gods and men.[15]

3. Women, by nature more libidinous than men, cannot be trusted in widowhood to maintain the essential celibacy.

Thus, the preservation of ritual status of all men in a clan (a division of a tribe) rested always on the behavior of any one woman in it. In explaining this belief, Veena Das, a member of the Bengal Legislative Assembly 1946–1951, writes: "Women were literally seen as points of entrance, as 'gateways' to the caste system." She adds that male sexuality did not threaten the clan's purity.[16] (Probably the founders saw male license as impossible to control in a warrior society.)

Clearly, a number of factors fed the unquenchable fires. Wives did elect to die to gain eternal union with their mate. Wives could be pressured by their families and custom. They could face a future so bleak that they preferred to die.

But wholesale conjugal fidelity? British records imply otherwise. It seems clear that a corpse's great wealth and high rank often mandated a suitably impressive number of Satis. The funeral in 1780 of the Raja of Narwar summoned 64 women to the pyre. Shortly thereafter a Punjabi prince was appeased in death by his ten wives and a drove of concubines. In 1843, the Maharaja Man Singh was suitably supplied with multiple Satis. Later, as European influence increased, slave girls were sometimes "induced" to replace reluctant wives.

On a wholesale basis, sati can only have been fed by what philosophers of both East and West have recognized as man's deadliest, most prevalent weakness—fierce-burning pride.

NOTES

1. P. Thomas, *Indian Women through the Ages* (New York: Asia Publishing House, 1864), p. 296.

2. Anant Sadashiv Altekar, *The Position of Women in Hindu Civilization,* 2nd ed. (Delhi- Motilal Banarsidass, 1973), p. 139.

3. Thomas, p. 296.

4. Stephen A. Tyler, *India: An Anthropological Perspective* (Pacific Palisades, Calif.: Goodyear, 1973), p. 196.

5. Thomas, p. 228.

6. Tyler, p. 135. Ramabai (see below) quotes seven references like the following from Manu, whom she says "all Hindus with few exceptions believe implicitly ... about women (p. 52): 'It is the nature of women to seduce men in this world; for that reason the wise are never unguarded in the company of females.'"

7. Altekar, p. 51.

8. Tyler, p. 136.

9. Quoted by three authorities: Altekar, Hopkins, and Ramabai.

10. Tyler, p. 136.

11. Altekar, p. 126.

12. Altekar, p. 137.

13. Pundita Ramabai, *The High-Caste Hindu Woman* (Philadelphia: Jas. B. Rodgers, 1887), p. 81. Several authorities, including the *Encyclopedia Britannica* (13th ed.), bear out the corruption of the Rig-veda. Ramabai, a Brahman and a college Professor of Sanskrit, writes thus: "It was by falsifying a single syllable [angre-agneh] that the unscrupulous priests managed to change entirely the meaning of the whole verse."

14. Tyler, p. 148.

15. Tyler, p

16. Veena Das, "Indian Women: Work, Power, and Status," in *Indian Women from Purdah to Modernity,* ed. B. R. Nanda (New Delhi: Vikas Publishing House, 1976), p. 135.

BIBLIOGRAPHY

Altekar, Anant Sadashiv. *The Position of Women in Hindu Civilization.* 2nd. Ed. Delhi: Motilal Banarsidass, 1973.

Cormack, Margaret Lawson. *The Hindu Woman.* New York: Bureau of Publications, Teachers College, Columbia University, 1953.

Das, Veena. "Indian Women: Work, Power, and Status," in *Indian Women from Purdah to Modernity.* ed. B. R. Nanda. New Delhi: Vikas Publishing House, 1976.

Hopkins, Saleni Armstrong. *Within the Purdah.* New York: Eaton & Mains, 1898.

Ramabai, Pundita. *The High-Caste Hindu Woman.* Philadelphia: Jas. B. Rodgers, 1887.

Rice, Edward. *The Ganges: A Personal Encounter.* New York: Four Winds, 1974.

Thomas, P. *Indian Women through the Ages.* New York: Asia Publishing House, 1964.

Tyler, Stephen A. *India: An Anthroplogical Perspective.* Pacific Palisades, California. Goodyear, 1973.

Walker, George Benjamin. *The Hindu World.* New York: Praeger, 1968.

SUMMARY

The combined templates often deepen your perception of your material. Moreover, the use of such a grid aids you at three stages of preparing a long paper: As you read, it cuts down the chore of writing notes. As you work out your structure tree, it simplifies organization. As you write, you'll find that to produce three short essays is less stressful than to labor through one that seems interminable.

We quote from others' material for three reasons: to give credit to the writer's achievement, to support facts that otherwise might be doubted, and to borrow a particularly effective phrase.

Rather than quote an undue number of sentences, it is often better to paraphrase, that is, to cast the material in your own words.

Footnotes, bibliography, and the formal outline all follow traditional requirements that should be checked to insure the correctness of the formal library report.

ASSIGNMENTS

1. From the material on the career of the jury consultant brought out by the grid, formulate a thesis sentence having a proof phrase. Then work out a structure tree exactly as if you were planning to write an essay on that topic.

2. Go through the original paragraph on the caste system in India that we used for paraphrasing. Strike out all unnecessary words and phrases, leaving only the subject and key verbs in each sentence. Then, without referring to the paraphrase, rewrite the facts in your own words.

3. After you have read the sati essay carefully, answer the following questions.

WHAT IT IS SECTION

Par. 1   a. Introductions should be packed with facts. Jot down briefly each separate detail (not just sentences) conveyed in this introductory paragraph.

b. In your own words, rephrase the thesis statement as a question that the body of the paper must answer.

Par. 2   a. Are the facts implied by the topic sentence supported?

Par. 3   a. What thought links the first two sentences?

b. The fourth sentence begins with the phrase "For *other* reasons." What is the first reason, implied rather than stated?

c. What is achieved by the last sentence? Is it necessary?

Par. 4   a. In the first sentence, why is the word *apparently* required?

b. Should another sentence be added to the paragraph? Why or why not?

Par. 5   a. Four of the five sentences begin with a prepositional phrase. For what reason?

b. All sentences present a passive verb. That is, the real subject does not appear; the original object has become the subject. Can you find two reasons for using passive verbs in this case?

WHY IT WORKED

Par. 6   a. What purpose is served by this short paragraph?

Par. 7   a. Which four words express the cause for which the final sentence is the result?

Par. 8   a. Which words indicate the two factors of the contrast?

b. List the image-making words.

Par. 9   a. What is the relationship between Paragraphs 8 and 9? How are the two similar in structure? Where else in this section is there similar structure?

b. Find a balanced sentence.

c. Note the handling of the quoted material. Is it economical?

Par. 10   a. While short, clear words are often more effective than Latinate expressions, what would be lost if "good" and "evil" were substituted for "beneficent" and "malevolent"? Read aloud both versions.

Par. 11   a. What metaphors are employed?

b. The last sentence represents what relationship to its predecessors?

c. What organizational purpose does it serve?

WHAT IT ACHIEVED

Par. 12   a. Find several suggested images. Are they effective?

Par. 13   a. In a good dictionary you will find *noblesse oblige,* even though it is a French expression. What are its implications for this section?

Par. 16   a. Underline key phrases that make this a forceful paragraph.

Par. 17   a. Most of us misuse the word *terrible*. What is the difference between "I have a terrible headache" and this paragraph's "terrible irony?" What is the irony?

Par. 19   In the last sentence, what purpose is served by the introduction of the almost meaningless phrase "of course?" Omit it, and then read the sentence.

Par. 20   Why is the last sentence phrased as a question?

Par. 21   a. What is gained by the wording "rests on a tripod of facts" rather than "results from three causes"? Why are the three reasons listed instead of appearing in the paragraph?

Par. 22   a. Try putting "always" ahead of "rested" and then read both versions aloud.
b. Account for the intended effect of the details supplied for Veena Das.

Par. 23   a. Can you account for the wording of each sentence in this paragraph? Why are they quite short?

Par. 24   a. How is transition achieved between Paragraphs 23 and 24?
b. What form of development underlies these sentences? What is their intended effect? Which word in the quoted sentence has the force of "terrible irony"?

Par. 25   a. Is the last sentence necessary? Would the article be improved by its omission?

Overall   In several different paragraphs, match the points that appear to those on the outline. Is any given point represented by more than one sentence? By less than one sentence? What do your answers suggest about the number of facts represented by a point on the outline?

4. *A Special Writing Project.* While most students acquire sufficient material for a long paper from their reading, it is also possible to develop a writing project from conducting a modified poll. In such a project you prepare a brief questionnaire and conduct interviews, either on the telephone (by a random choice from the directory) or in person by going door-to-door.

As a writing project, such a poll delivers several advantages. Whether or not you are at ease with strangers, you do benefit from talking to assorted types of people, and any shyness is eased by having set questions to ask them. Moreover, the ability to conduct interviews is a highly useful skill. (You might offer your paper to a local newspaper.) In addition, if you have chosen your topic carefully, you will learn invaluable information about your fellow citizens.

The choice of a topic and the preparation of the questionnaire require careful consideration along these lines:

a. *Subject.* Choose a subject about which there is sure to be a division of opinion and some strong reactions. A good possibility is the death penalty.

b. *Questions.* Word all questions on the questionnaire sheet so that they can be answered by a check in the yes-no box. (You might arrange to have the school computer tabulate the results.) The questions should be grouped to anticipate the usual answers. (This stage requires some forethought and study.) Keep the questions free from bias; in asking them, try to remain neutral.

c. *Back-up Questions.* Keep in mind the need to obtain information *in addition to* the statistics, about which you can write only so much. Lead your interviewees to talk about their reasons for the opinions they've voiced; it is these special observations that support the points your essay presents. Keep paper on your clipboard on which you can jot down details *after* concluding the interview.

d. *Choosing Interviewees.* The paper will benefit considerably if you set up a possible conflict: the answers given in one neighborhood as opposed to another; the opinions of middle-aged people as opposed to those of people under thirty.

NOTES

1. Dennie Van Tassel, *Program Style, Design, Efficiency, Debugging, and Testing,* 2nd ed. (Englewood Cliffs, N.J.: Prentice-Hall, Inc., 1978) pp. 63, 64.

2. Van Tassel, p. 47.

3. Pundita Ramabai, *The High-Caste Hindu Woman* (Philadelphia: Jas. B. Rogers, 1887), pp. 6-7.

9
MANAGING
MANAGERIAL
WRITING

Goal: To learn the basics of successful executive corresponence and its strategies

Just what is managerial writing?

We shall consider the term sufficiently elastic to cover a wide area: the everyday writing required of administrators, executives, supervisors, vice-presidents—management in general.

If we exclude highly technical reports that include tables and abstruse symbols, their communication seems to fall into three broad groups, according to the problem to be solved. These we classify by the relationships of the three essentials involved—reader, writer, and problem. The first group—general correspondence—becomes the concern of this chapter. (By problem, we mean the subject matter or situation that motivates the communication—not just the benefits of a product or service, a complaint, the established policy, but also the underlying purpose of reports of various kinds, manuals of instructions, a good many documents.)

What these two chapters will *not* include is what is commonly meant in the phrase "business writing." That is, we shall *not* refer to the mechanics of correctness. Such rules are essential but beyond our domain. We seek to program your reader to think a certain way—your way. Thus, we shall be concerned with analysis, point of view, strategies. As the title of this chapter suggests, the careful application of the principles you find here will enable you to control your writing, to derive benefits from it, to turn communication into an asset. According to an article in *Harvard Business Review,* "What Helps or Harms Promotability"

(January 1964), at the top of the list of twenty-two attributes considered by top corporations for executive promotion stands "good communication skills."

All in all, if in the following quotation we let "sound facts" correspond to "numeric values," our concerns will be precisely those that Marian Bohl establishes for computer programmers:

> One of the most widely applied measures of program performance is quality of output—precision and accuracy of numeric values, appropriateness and level of content, readability, understandability, timeliness, and so on. ... In short, it is thinking errors, more than coding errors [the symbols that correspond to grammar and punctuation in our writing] that limit programmer productivity.[1]

Please do not begin your study of managerial writing with this chapter. Only if you have allotted considerable thought to the foundation established in the eight preceding chapters can you build additional skills. Good writing, Hemingway said, is a matter of architecture, not of interior decoration. Writers of top-level managerial communication will agree.

THREE CLASSES OF MANAGERIAL WRITING

There is an incredible variety of communication suggested in our chosen term. Necessarily, then, we over-simplify. After some investigation, we find it logical to divide managerial writing into three simple classes, each with its own requirements for good handling. A large proportion of general writing falls into these categories.

1. *Person A addresses Person B to solve a problem, either A's or B's.* This situation represents the bulk of person-to-person correspondence. *A* writes *B* (whom he knows or purports to know) to sell him something or to ask something from him. In most cases A's self-interest is at stake; therefore, B's favorable state of mind is the determining factor.

2. *Person A addresses a problem; his writing is to be read by X^x.* Here we have an even broader spectrum. It can range from the sonorous phrasing of an official report to an explanation of the price of gold as it affects the world's economy. As we intend it, however, it is the impersonal situation in which a writer prepares material to be read by any number of strangers who, for various reasons, cannot be addressed by the informal *you*. The emphasis rests primarily on the focused subject, the problem.

3. *Person A addresses a problem to be implemented by C^x.* This situation shades into both its predecessors. It is most often internal rather than external communication—someone in a company writing a handbook for other employees; rules for company property; instructions of various kinds. *A* may or may not know the *C*'s who will read his material, although he knows much about them.

Thus, our three groups are determined by basic questions: Is the reader a prime mover? Or is the reader unknown, so that the problem becomes the entire focus? Or again, is the reader the agent who will actually handle the problem?

Such questions begin the process of analysis that results in successful communication in the market-place.

APPLICATION OF PAST PRINCIPLES

As we have said, the concern of this chapter is that of Group 1, general correspondence. While all three groups continue to require the principles presented thus far, this group depends on them most heavily. In college, you wrote for your teacher as reader, in order to earn a grade. Similarly, in general correspondence you write for one reader, in order to earn money. Thus, you'll find it helpful to review the basic principles and to note the heightened emphasis on the reader.

STRENGTHS TO MAINTAIN

Cover Sentence	*Yes.* This expression of your main thought belongs in the first paragraph of every letter or memo. Traditionally, a given letter discusses only one topic (for filing purposes).
Structure tree	*Yes.* If managerial correspondence weighs more heavily with you than academic essays, then planning *on paper* becomes that much more critical.
Algorithm	*Yes.* You owe it to yourself to present your ideas in the most accessible order.
Developmental processes	Comparison/contrast, analogy, definition, cause/result—because they are logical, they are important.
Transitions	Smooth-flowing prose bespeaks professionalism and calm reasoning—the kind of thoughtful control that characterizes a good executive.
Choice of words	*Yes.* The friendly, knowledgeable tone you convey is most important; to the reader, you *are* the company you represent.

CHANGES TO CONSIDER

Corporate image	You're no longer operating singly; you're writing for two, yourself *and* your employer. A company's corporate image is often its best—and most costly—stock in trade.
Importance of first paragraph	All business communication should begin with an overview (which is usually the cover sentence). If your message is good news, let it ring bells; if it is bad, modify the blow, but convey it nevertheless—regretfully.
Paragraphing	Brief paragraphs provide white space that mean heightened readability. You should consider paragraphing at every node of your structure tree.

Proof phrase	Obviously, your message dictates the number of points you introduce—not always a triad.

THE THREE-P TEMPLATE

To cope with the divisions of managerial writing, we shall provide you with a useful template that consists of a set of WH-questions. In writing Group 1 communication, these questions will center on the reader (whose response will solve the problem). In Group 3, the same questions will be addressed to the problem, and in a different order of importance.

We need a name for this adjustable template—a mnemonic device by which you will avoid confusing it with our earlier What-it-is template. Because all three groups are based on *p*-words, we shall dub our template the Three-P template. In the first set (with which this chapter will be concerned), we use the Who-for version; in the third (which we delay until the following chapter, along with Group 2), we apply the What-for, as you will see. Probably *your* writing is most concerned with one or the other, not both. Executives who write correspondence usually do not write manuals of instructions and vice versa; writers of pamphlets and the like ordinarily do not handle official correspondence. Thus, the template will present no confusion of versions.

The Who-for Version

No reasonably complicated correspondence can be organized until the writer has thoroughly examined the point of view of the person addressed. His desired response constitutes the problem to which the communication is addressed. Unless it means nothing to you, you should consider the strategy needed to evoke a desirable reaction.

Here is a triad of questions to ask, our person-to-person template. It is slightly ungrammatical—but who would have remembered "Winston tastes good as a cigarette should"?

Who for?
What for?
Why for?

These brief questions cue you to ask others they suggest:

For whom	is this message? Who is he? Your superior? Your subordinate? A customer? What are his limitations? Will he understand your technical terms? Will he be favorably inclined?
What	information does he need? Have you analyzed your material in terms of his needs? Are you giving him enough facts? Are you wasting his time and attention by giving him unnecessary or imprecise material?
Why	does he need this material? For what purpose will he use it? Is he to take some action, come to some decison? Is the action essential?

The purpose of the template is this: to remind you to push beyond your personal concerns in order to find and focus on your reader's needs. This Golden Rule is not only ethical; it is realistic and highly practical. If you dismiss it as elementary or unnecessary, consider the sad story of an account executive who overlooked the real purpose of a client's request.

On the brink of a heavy regional advertising campaign, the retiring president of the sponsoring Midwestern farm implements company called its New York agency to request a last-minute change in copy approved earlier. The change involved replacing the company's familiar acronym with the full title represented by the initials, including the old man's last name. The account executive, ascribing the request to simple vanity, explained that, in view of the time element, such a change was impossible. "Well, check it out with your boss," the old man insisted.

But the agency head was in Canada on a hunting trip, and the account man, sure of his response, decided against placing the call.

Shortly after the agency head returned, however, he called the account executive in and fired him. "You should have remembered that the old man's son was planning to run for Congress," the boss said grimly. "He wanted the TV spots to do double duty—to sell both the product and the family name. You should have worked out some compromise, or called me."

It's easy to *assume* what the reader wants or needs; applying the template *assures* that you view your communication from where he stands.

REAL-LIFE WRITING: IAN KEITH AND THE REVERSED FLAGS

Let's apply the Who-for template to a specific problem.

To tie in with the first visit of the Princess of Wales to this country, a large East Coast department store chain is introducing a line of Princess Di fashions. Along with a lavish fashion show in each store using Diana look-alikes, animated window displays, and gift pictures, the stores have ordered special glossy white merchandise bags and boxes imprinted with the bright-colored crossed flags of the two countries.

We are the well-known printing firm responsible for handling those bags, and in keeping with such an important order, we've checked every step of the process. As the big cartons are being loaded on trucks for shipment, right on time, one of the older pressmen comes in with a discard he's picked up.

"Aren't the flags on this thing reversed?" he asks mildly.

"I don't know," the office manager answers. "Why? Does it make any difference?"

"Sure does ... There's rules for those things."

It develops that he's right on both counts. There are rules, and the flags *are* reversed. The American flag should be on its own right. More important, in the authorized original, the flags were correctly placed, the American flag's staff over the British staff.

Now what?

Obviousy, we must persuade Ian Keith, the stores' promotion head, to accept the mistake. On this $11,000 order, our costs are $8,000, and we can't send that down the drain.

We decide that it is more strategic to write a letter than to phone. Because Ian Keith will need time to consider the situation, we don't want to risk his first hasty decision.

Now we settle down to apply the Who-for template.

WHO FOR *(FOR WHOM ARE WE WRITING?)*

Keith—oldish, late 50's. World War II veteran. Not the expansive type usually found in promotion, but meticulous, scrupulously exact about everything. Takes pride in having come up the hard way. He'd be an enemy for life to anyone who set out to trick him. Still, his practical experience must have taught him that mistakes happen everywhere.

WHAT FOR *(WHAT DOES HE NEED?)*

He needs the whole truth, expressed without excuse or lavish apologies. He will expect financial restitution commensurate with whatever damage he suffers.

WHY *(WHY DOES HE NEED IT?)*

He needs to save face, his own and his company's. Because the responsibility lies at his door, he needs a good answer to pass on to his superiors. Undoubtedly he will send a copy of our letter to them.

Let's see how these answers work for us.

From the notes we make in answer to *who,* we can determine the stance we shall take—no excuses, a sincere apology that acknowledges just what such a mistake can mean in a costly promotion. No flippancy, no breast-beating. We won't say we were rushed, because we weren't, as he knows. Even if we had been, we actively solicit rush work. We won't say that we've fired the guilty supervisor.

Now for *what.* After discussion, we agree that we'll offer a discount amounting to our profit. We'll simply bill him for our cost, without mentioning its basis.

As for *why,* we can help him save face by reminding his superiors that we have a reputation for dependability. We'll say that, except for the time element, we would rerun the order. We'll slip in some adroit praise for the promotion, which may have been Keith's idea.

Of course, we acknowledge the inadequacy of such answers. While we can absolve Keith, we are still concerned with the stores' real need to save face. If only we had some sweetener other than the discount! We call in some of the people from sales for brainstorming.

For a while, nothing sounds feasible. Then the senior partner speaks up. "We need to turn this thing inside out. Make a liability into an asset."

Blankly, we ponder this possibility.

The senior partner—a gray-haired, paunchy oldster much like Ian Keith, begins slowly to spin out an idea. "This flag design was checked repeatedly, and nobody caught the mistake." He pauses. "So why don't we urge Keith to make use of the error as a promotion? I mean, well—In the big spreads he'll run in the papers, he could mention a printing error customers will find at the store . . . The first ten people who discover that error will get a prize—Merchandise, a discount, or whatever."

One of the saleswomen leans forward in her enthusiasm, gesturing approval. "Make the prize a pair of leather gloves! Princess Di is fond of gloves—"

The senior partner glances around; all faces show approval. "I figured we'd pay for the prize—at cost, of course."

A copywriter speaks up. "You know what? I bet the newspapers would run a feature on it. Point up the public's ignorance about the flag—that sort of thing. And it's an ingenious way to solve a problem."

"Right," someone else chimes in. "Maybe some local Boy Scout will come up first. The paper might even run a picture."

The meeting breaks up on an upbeat of enthusiasm.

Now we have to write that all-important letter. It's not hard to plan; we'll keep it short—one page—and to the point.

First comes the overview. (*All* business correspondence should begin with an overview, remember.) We'll mention first all the pluses: The order went out on the scheduled date. The printing itself is sharp and clear, the colors just right. Now we come to the problem. The cover sentence. We must acknowledge the error, yet be reassuring. In effect, we'll gently suggest trouble ahead, but immediately refer to a means of handling it.

Why must we divulge the problem, instead of working into it gradually?

It's a much-written law of business correspondence that you owe your reader a preview of what's to come. Busy officials have a right to know why you ask their time to read your message.

Now for our strategic organization. We could, of course, state the problem in the second paragraph, and in the third, our solution. There's the matter of pace, however. If Keith rushes through in one quick spurt, his reaction may not be favorable. We must give him time to appreciate our offer. We'll build to a climax.

Each of our paragraphs becomes a stage in the development of our production:

Preview
Problem

Build-up (partial solution)
Solution (climax)
Conclusion (clincher)

Not only does our organization reflect strategy, but our tone must be similarly planned. In the letter that follows, see if you can discover the devices we use. When you have succeeded, you will find the annotated letter reproduced at the end of the chapter.

Mr. Ian Keith
Sales Promotion
Saxe & Coburg Stores
New York, N. Y.

Dear Ian:

Our printing of Saxe & Coburg bags and boxes has gone out today as planned, ready for your Princess Di promotion.

You will agree that the job looks excellent. The colors are a good match, including the gold of the staffs. In one minor aspect only does the work differ from your specifications, and we think the advantages associated with this change will outweigh your reservations.

In the kind of glitch that's visited on all printers, the imprint of the two flags was reversed throughout. Unlike you, our people here were not aware of the requirements governing the flag's proper display. Thus, the error was not caught until today, too close to your deadline for us to rerun the order.

Perhaps you will agree that the plan we have devised—plus a healthy 20% discount—will counterbalance this regrettable mistake. Why not capitalize on the public's newsworthy ignorance with an in-store promotion?

On opening day, what if you offered a prize of a pair of leather gloves to the first ten customers who track down your printer's error? (We understand the Princess favors gloves.) A couple of lines in your newspaper ads, plus placards inside the entrance doors—that would set it up. We'll pay for ten pairs of gloves for each store at about $20 your cost.

Again, we greatly regret what happened. We hope that, rather than detracting from your impressive Princess Di promotion, our change will contribute in a small way to its certain success.

Sincerely,

STRATEGIES
OF MANAGERIAL WRITING

A letter like that to Keith, we think, is what managerial writing is all about. Such writing offers the challenge of competition so dear to the American businessman. It resembles a chess game, an alternation of moves toward a desired result. Managerial writing of this kind is more exciting to plan than the ploys of advertising, for the copywriter must launch his message out into the blue, not knowing whom it will reach.

The devices with which you play this game are diction (the choice of language) and structure (the elements of a sentence or larger section of writing). They are the wherewithal of emphasis. As the *person-to-person template* makes clear, the writer's emphasis should slant toward the reader. (He is the person being programmed, remember.) Such a slant does not come naturally to many individuals, whose thoughts cluster around *I, me, my* when writing, as opposed to the necessary *you* and *your*. (Remember the short-sighted account executive.)

Let's look over the shoulder of the personnel manager of one of Saxe & Coburg's stores. With two applications for employment on his desk, he is considering a choice between two young women for an apprenticeship to the store's fashions buyer. As the girls wait for their interviews, his secretary directs each one to write 100 words or so on her reason for wanting the job.

Which of the following letters do you think will impress the personnel manager more favorably?

IMOGENE'S LETTER

I am applying for this position because I have always liked clothes and I think I would be happy working in fashions.

I am told I have good taste, and I can tell when a person would look good in certain styles and colors. (My friends and family often take my advice.)

While I know the beginning salary is not what I had expected as a college graduate, I understand that I can expect regular raises as I move up, which I am sure I will do.

ROSIE'S LETTER

Ever since I can remember, Saxe & Coburg has represented a sort of fairyland to me. It is so impressively big—and yet its people always seem unfailingly friendly and helpful.

Many times, when I have been "just looking" at your new fashions, obviously beyond my pocketbook, your salespeople have chatted with me about my continuing interest in clothes—about trends, which brand-names you favor, and the guidelines used by your buyers.

After having drawn a composite of the typical Saxe & Coburg second-floor customer, I think I know her kind of person very well. If you award me the apprenticeship, I shall concentrate on deepening her trust in Saxe & Coburg.

It's possible, of course, that an employer would prefer the aggressive, self-confident Imogene. (But note the implications of the parenthetical sentence in the second paragraph. Is there a difference implied in the verb *take,* as opposed to *ask?*) Almost every clause includes the subject *I.* Would an employee so obviously self-centered work well with other employees? What about her attitude toward salary? Will she soon become dissatisfied with her paycheck and quit?

In Rosie's letter, note the more modest sentences, the orientation toward the store itself, the complimentary, ingenuous linking of the personnel manager with the great corporation. Rosie subtly suggests the desirable attitude of the salespeople toward young browsers (who in a few years may become good customers), as well as her own appealing personality.

Moreover, this writer indicates that she has done her homework, although she does not boast of it. It appears that she has given this extra effort, not as a means of weighting her application, but wholly from her interest in such work. In her implied relationship to the store, she seems aware of a basic rule in business and industry: The employer expects profit not only from his capital investments, but from his investment in each employee.

The second letter, then, lays as much emphasis as possible on the future employer, something not easy to do in a job application. Here, the slant of interest away from the writer is achieved by maintaining the store's point of view wherever possible. Nevertheless, Rosie manages to convey a very favorable impression of herself and her abilities.

In addition to such devices as Rosie presents, other kinds of emphasis are achieved by manipulation of sentence elements.

1. *Placement of key words.* As we have noted before, phrases placed at the end of a sentence generally receive the most force, although those at the beginning also have impact. Thus, any bad news can be minimized by burying it between facts more acceptable to the reader.

2. *A pause before and after a key phrase.* Because we are taught to read quickly, snatching up groups of words at a time, anything that signals a pause for a special group acts to underline it.

Consider the reference to the reduced cost of the printing offered in the letter to Keith.

> Perhaps you will agree that the plan we have devised—plus a healthy 20% discount—will counterbalance this regrettable mistake.

Incidentally, in this sentence the use of the dash as opposed to the comma renders the interpolated phrase more dramatic in implication.

While we advise against separating the subject from its verb, or the verb from its object, the insertion of an "interrupter" that is cut off by commas lends emphasis to the phrases that follow.

> The jury decided, however, that he was guilty on all counts but the first.
> The solution, we find, is that the legacy be split equally between the two cousins.
> The only thing to do, then, is to carry on.

A warning must accompany this device: It is easy to work into a writing rhythm that causes you continually to interrupt your sentences needlessly. Be sure to save such interruptions for situations where emphasis belongs.

3. *Reversal*. Another form of emphasis in sentence structure is achieved by switching ends of a sentence, or pulling out a word from the middle in order to place it at the beginning.

    a. His college years lay behind him.
    b. Behind him lay his college years.

    a. Test scores had never soared so high.
    b. Never had test scores soared so high.

    a. The plunge into the real world lies ahead of every college student.
    b. Ahead of every college student lies the plunge into the real world.

    a. That he was nervous was obvious.
    b. It was obvious that he was nervous.

4. *Parallelism*. You can emphasize a group of elements by shaping them in similar form and then calling attention to their parallelism, either by numbering or by the use of dots called "bullets." In the following example from an insurance company folder, both the repetition of introductory words and the eye-catching bullets device emphasize the choices available to the borrower.

To repay the loan, you have three choices:

- You may make payments directly to the Company at your convenience.

- You may authorize us to draw on your checking account each month.

- You may make your loan payments with your premium payments.

In a professional report (as in an essay), the logic of the formal outline is demonstrated by the parallelism of its noun phrases (or sentences). (You may wish to review the formal outline for "The Ladies for the Burning" in Chapter 8.) Similarities of indentation, notation, and phrasing indicate similarities in importance of the various divisions.

Parallelism within sentence structure is a favorite device of the accomplished writer. For the person who is unacquainted with sentence elements, it may present some grammatical difficulties.

5. *White space*. To call attention to a critical element, you may frame it in more white space than you allow to other elements. A single sentence may become a paragraph, or a paragraph may be indented further than its fellows.

6. *Repetition of a key word*. In protesting a seller's disregard of contractural obligations, for example, the customer's letter of complaint could repeat the words "The contract says" more often than is necessary. For another example, see the letter from the Vice President for Advertising reproduced on page 156.

THE PROBLEMS WITH DICTATION

To make sure our letter to Ian Keith represented the best possible version of our strategy, we carefully planned it and then sketched it out in longhand.

The reluctance to plan *on paper*—coupled with the immediate availability of dictating—probably accounts for the preponderance of unorganized, poorly expressed managerial communication. Instead of planning first and then dictating, many businessmen combine thinking and uttering as a simultaneous process. The ease with which an executive can open his mouth and issue rambling sentences is a temptation to which many succumb.

Perhaps such a person reasons this way:

"I'm a pretty smart cookie to be holding down this position. That means I can think, right? Okay, so my time is worth money. Which counts more—spending the company's time on everyday correspondence, or spieling off what I'm thinking about? After all, executives aren't supposed to be English teachers. Write the way you'd talk; that's my line of reference."

Intelligence is not equated with the ability to speak as if you had prewritten your material. At a small private college recently, a nationally-recognized scholar made a Founders Day address from notes. The slant of his message pleased the college president so much that he had the tape recording transcribed and a copy of the speech sent to all faculty members.

In reading the material, some of the faculty were amazed at the contrast between their favorable reaction to the speech as voiced, and the reservations they now felt toward what they saw in writing. The scholar's opening metaphor remained striking; his clear, logical points manifested a planned development. The sentences in which he had expressed them, however, were rambling and full of empty syllables, linked with *and*'s and *so*'s. His diction was entirely conversational. Perhaps the greatest loss of potential appeared in his conclusion, where he failed to tie in with his opening metaphor, a means of underlining his message.

The point is this: What is spoken, whether in a speech or in dictation, does not always transfer well when it is put in writing.

While the scholar's speech was subject to criticism, it is likely that he could and did dictate very well. He had written a number of books, and he was in communication with top-level government officials. Unlike him, many of us dictate no better than we can speak without a script. Because dictation is an everyday essential in business, not many top-level executives see it as the culprit in weak communication.

Not long ago, a well-known paper products company arranged for a college English teacher to conduct a writing course for its middle-management people. On an initial tour of the well-equipped building, the teacher was conducted to an office termed the Communications Center. From recording apparatus, a number of women were typing correspondence on word processors, wonderful machines that produced every possible aid to perfection.

"Our phones serve as dictation recorders," the guide explained proudly. "The executives need only pick up the phone and begin to talk!"

She handed the teacher a large, handsome red booklet of instructions. In gold letters two inches high, the ironic title fairly leaped at the teacher: *Don't write—dictate!*

Of course, dictation and good writing need not be mutually exclusive. How, then, do you learn to dictate well?

Only by thinking and planning ahead and, after dictating, checking back. As the guide at the paper company explained, the person dictating can call at any time for a playback. Even the book of instructions for using the dictation system emphasizes the need for a rough draft in preparing important communication. When that is typed and returned to the executive, he should make the necessary adjustments, then read out the corrected material.

While this may be done in some situations, often it is omitted by those who need most to learn the skills of dictating. Not only are they loath to spend the additional time, but they feel that if they make a practice of changing what they have dictated, they betray incompetency or lose face with the typists.

(It is said that, in certain industries, executives are reluctant to keep a computer in their offices; it too closely resembles a typewriter.)

Here is a typical letter that shows the weaknesses of dictation, even by an M.B.A. from a prestigious school. As manager of a plant that makes dairy product containers, he voices the proverbial conflict between the home office and sales in an angry protest to the sales manager. You can see him, red-faced and glowering, as he picks up his microphone and begins to dictate:

> Bill, several times that I know of I have warned you guys in Sales about this problem. Maybe it was Pete I talked to, but anyway you knew about it.
>
> You positively must check out new-product prices with this office. This morning I was placed in the ridiculous position of seeming not to know our current prices. An order came in that was shown to me for a carload of the new pyramid containers, citing only a 7% rise in cost. That is the figure for the test area, yes, but it is not the rise of 9% that has been decided on by this office. Of course, I called Richest to point out the error in their figures, and of course they told me that you had assured them last month that the 6% Greenville price would hold. Of course, I assured them that we would honor your commitment, but you can bet I don't appreciate being made to look like a fool.
>
> I hope you see that you assumed too much authority in your concern to please a good customer. Another time, you should remember that you must clear any price change with this department.

You will note that the writer remembered to provide an overview, although it does not contain the cover sentence (the first sentence in the second paragraph). From the wording of that overview, it is clear that he has plunged into dictation without taking time to consider what that overview should contain. Instead of an early, clear reference to the specific situation that is his cause for writing, he deals with his own experience rather than with the information his reader needs. He is so concerned with his loss of face that not until halfway through the letter does he provide the name of the customer (Richest), a matter of chief concern to his reader.

You may question the repetition of the phrase "of course." You have probably heard that a good writer finds synonyms wherever possible. Under some circumstances, that is true. Here, the second "of course" might suggest a certain inattention. But by the third—can't you hear the teeth-grinding sarcasm?

Richard Sheridan, a famous playwright, said that "easy writing's vile hard reading." With that in mind, picture the purchasing agent of a small leasing company as he suddenly notices an error in printing that he should have caught months ago. In his embarrassment, he picks up his dictation microphone and issues the following letter to the supplier:

> I have only now found out that the novelty date books we ordered from you last year have our company name misspelled. We have been handing them out during the past months without noticing that error, so now we have only 204 of the original order left, which you can understand we don't want to use. The name should have been printed Marley-Kayle Leasing Company, but somehow it came out as Marley-Kaile as you can see by the one I enclose. I don't know precisely the number ordered previously, but presently we are cutting down on the number of giveaways, so you can quote me a price on just 300 of these novelty date books properly printed.

What mental picture do you form of this writer? Shouldn't he ask for credit for the misprints when he makes a new order? A better verison of this letter might read thus:

> Please quote us a price on 300 novelty date books like the one enclosed.
>
> You'll note that in our last order our firm name was misspelled. Since we must discard the 204 we now have in stock, we would appreciate credit for that number applied to our next order.

Do we need to point out the exact error in spelling? No, our letter is written on letterhead stationery. We need only refer to the mistake, not belabor it.

The same purchasing agent wrote the following letter. Obviously, he fails to sort out in his mind what needs to be said and in what order:

> We ordered six dozen calendars earlier this month at a special price of $.43 each. Now it turns out that we will need seven dozen instead of six because of an error in planning. I am enclosing a purchase order for the extra dozen calendars, therefore, to be stamped with the Marley-Kayle Leasing Company name in red, and I hope you can allow us the same low price, which will be much appreciated.

One sentence will convey the necessary information more efficiently:

> Please send an extra dozen calendars like the six dozen we ordered earlier this month, preferably at the same price of $.43 each.

For such simple letters, of course, it is not necessary to plan on paper. Certainly, however, the purchasing agent should have organized his thoughts in order to produce a concise statement.

How well do such letters represent the company image? If the purchasing agent were investigated for promotion, how would such material reflect—not just his writing ability—but his thought processes?

SUMMARY

The written communication expected of executives can be classified in three broad classes: person-to-person about a problem; person-to-problem-to person; and person-to-problem-to-subordinate. To cope with the first, you should analyze your correspondent, his needs, and his expectations. Focusing on these, you utilize the various strategies afforded by diction and structure to achieve the purpose of your letter. Such skillful expression is difficult to achieve in routine dictation; it requires planning on paper.

ASSIGNMENT

Let us say that you are Lieutenant Governor of the state of New Dakota, an elective position that normally means a shoo-in as Governor in the next election.

You have a shrewd and capable aide, Xeno Zeiglitsch, who is also an arrogant so-and-so, well aware that his family connections control a good-sized block of votes in a key county. In the past, as now, Xeno has an unpleasant tendency to throw his weight around. His latest misadventure has just now hit the headlines.

Recently when he was visiting Wintu Lake, a popular convention resort, his car was ticketed for parking in a no-parking zone. After Xeno ignored the $5 ticket on the state-owned vehicle, he received notice of a $10 late-penalty fee. He sent in a check for $10 to the Chief of Police of Wintu Lake, accompanied by a letter on official state stationery. Typed by his state-employee secretary, the letter indicated that a resort area so inconsiderate of an influential (underlined) visitor clearly did not deserve the two political conventions slated within the next six months. He therefore felt it incumbent on him to see that they were relocated in some city more appreciative of those who served their state.

In threatening to cancel the two conventions, Xeno assumes that he can wield *your* authority, for he is not well-liked by the state chairman, who has the final say. Nevertheless, you cannot afford to fire him. The most you can do is to see that your reprimand goes in his permanent record, where it can affect promotions and pay raises.

You, as Lieutenant Governor, must write three communications, copies of which will go to the news media: (1) a letter of apology to the Wintu Lake Chief of Police; (2) an official reprimand to Xeno; and (3) a news release that states your reaction to Xeno's misuse of authority.

Plan and write the letters, utilizing the strategies presented in this chapter.

The following annotated letter refers back to p. 148 and our discussion of strategy.

Mr. Ian Keith

Sales Promotion Manager

Saxe & Coburg Stores

New York, N.Y.

Dear Ian:

Use of firm name

Our printing of Saxe & Coburg bags and boxes has gone out today as planned, ready for your unique Princess Di promotion.

Praise for promotion.

Not *we*, but *you* as subject

You will agree that the job looks excellent. The colors are a good match, including the gold of the staffs. In one minor aspect only

Reassurance

Careful wording —quick cover-up.

does the work differ from your specifications, and we think the advantages associated with this change will outweigh your reservations.

Reminder—all printing is subject to such mistakes.

In the kind of glitch that's visited on all printers, the imprint of the two flags was reversed throughout. Unlike you, our people here were not aware of the requirements governing the flag's proper

Hidden subject (not *we* reversed).

His superior knowledge

We don't want this added loss.

display. Thus, the change was not caught until today, too close to your deadline for us to rerun the order.

Another acknowledgment of his superior information.

Perhaps you will agree that the plan we have devised—plus a healthy discount—will counterbalance this regrettable mistake. Why not capitalize on the public's newsworthy ignorance with an in-store promotion?

Pause before and after important fact.

We are specific about details

On opening day, what if you offered a prize of a pair of leather gloves to the first ten customers who track down your printer's error? (We understand the Princess favors gloves.) A couple of lines in your newspaper spreads, plus placards inside the entrances—that would set it up. We'll pay for ten pairs of gloves for each store at about $20 each, your cost.

He'll pick up the publicity angle as his idea.

The promotion will not involve extra expense

Ample apologies to satisfy him.

Again, we greatly regret this goof. It just might be that, rather than detracting from your impressive Princess Di promotion, our change will contribute in a small way to its certain success.

Happy ending

Sincerely,

NOTES

1. Marilyn Bohl, *A Guide for Programmers* (Englewood Cliffs, N.J.: Prentice-Hall, Inc., 1978) p. 28.

10
MAKING OBJECTIVE WRITING READABLE

GOAL: To alter an objective approach to the needs of unknown readers

In the first eight chapters we emphasized such principles as top-down organization, clarity, and sentence development.

In these two chapters on managerial writing—which build on that foundation—our emphasis focuses on job-related strategies of readability. As opposed to student writing that remains within the classroom, managerial writing wings forth to many readers who may criticize it, misunderstand it, and, if possible, not even read it. Obviously, then, most managerial writing needs to be reader-oriented.

Our preceding chapter divided readers into three groups, the first of which involved general correspondence, where readership is limited. The last two, the subject matter of this chapter, consider the reader as less immediate than the material, which is often treated with formal objectivity. Our contention holds that the reader is never incidental, that much of the wooden, dull obscurity found in this kind of writing can be made readable—and more effective—if certain rules for readability are observed.

Our two remaining groups are as follows:

2. Person *A* objectively addresses a problem; reader and writer are assumed and ignored.

Here, the professional writer seeks to present facts as he finds them to be, not as they may be slanted. If he steps into the report at all, it is in the section allotted to recommendations.

3. Person *A* addresses a problem, the solution of which must be carried out by underlings or personnel in other divisions.

Such notices and directives bulk large in internal corporate communication: restrictions and requirements of various kinds, memos, manuals of instruction, and so on. In our proliferation of state and federal governmental offices, one authority estimates that many officials spend more than half their time issuing such directives.

THE WEAKNESS
OF OVERBEARING OBJECTIVITY

As opposed to the subject *I* or *you,* objective writing emphasizes the inanimate subject it addresses. Its intention is to maintain the high, lofty plane of professionalism, to exclude human fallibility, and to address its material as though its tenets were emblazoned in gold on the heavens.

(Until recently, writing handbooks employed this level of address, so that writers found themselves adjuring students to avoid such practices as the passive, which they themselves were using. Now that human warmth proves to result in better learning, handbooks have descended from their pedestal.)

There is nothing inherently wrong with objective writing in itself; distressing examples furnished by those who deplore the practice simply result from what is poor writing in any style: jargon—when it is intended for non-professionals—inert verbs, nouns piled high as adjectives, abstractions at both ends of a sentence, trailing strings of prepositional phrases. (In this section thus far we have written objectively, avoiding personal pronouns and using formal diction. Probably you have noticed little difference.)

No doubt, objectivity's cold, impersonal tone originated in the ponderous verbosity of the law, as law-givers sought to cover all contingencies and to outdistance fear and favor. Early English laws deliberately voiced many expressions twice, once for the educated who knew Latinate expressions, and again for the working classes, whose heritage was short, blunt Anglo-Saxon (in reversed order: *last will and testament*).

From the law it found its way into bewildering insurance policies, banks' loan agreements, department stores' charge account terms, and so on. Today, however, such information must be stated subjectively, so that the average person will understand what he's signing.

As a sort of intellectual snobbery, objective writing has flooded the social sciences, education, and now technology. In each field, it has picked up such jargon that its communications resemble a set of secret languages, known to the initiate, as in secret societies.

So strongly deplored is psychologists' jargon, for example, that a *New York Times* book critic, Geoffrey Nunberg, reviewing *The Psychology of Literacy* by

Sylvia Scribner and Michael Cole (12/13/81), remarked that it was "astonishingly" lucid and readable to have been written by psychologists!

Dr. Herman M. Weisman of the National Bureau of Standards condemns the practice of convoluted jargon thus:

> The puerile practice of over-objectivity is probably the reason why scientific journals have become archival and professional scientific conferences have become too popular, even though oral communication is inherently less efficient than written communication.[1]

Note that expression *over*-objectivity. If professionals in a given field employ jargon among themselves, few outsiders would object. It is when they address others in the name of communication that objectivity receives its bad name.

Wordiness

Under the heading of "wordiness" we shall discuss two weaknesses that often appear in objective writing: sentences that are over-long, and circumlocution—phrasing that requires too many words to convey its meaning.

While very good sentences are written that extend to as many as forty words, far more are monsters that hook one clause to another until the reader is hopelessly confused.

Then how long is too long?

Readability experts base their pronouncements on the educational level of the readers you have in mind. The experts determine the ratio of words to education by various readability formulas, developed by years of tests and studies.

One such formula, developed by Robert Gunning, is known as the Fog Index. From a sample 100-word passage, it first determines the average number of difficult words and the number of words in the average sentence. In five simple operations, it arrives at a score—the number of years of schooling required for satisfactory comprehension of that kind of writing. In business and industry, corporations regularly have such tests run on material intended for the public.

Most authorities agree that an average of 15 to 18 words per sentence suits the general public. Any more than thirty for college people suggests the need for revision.

We'll touch briefly on circumlocution—a Latin derivative meaning "to speak in a roundabout way." To express your message in a direct way without unnecessary words is a major principle of good writing. All too often we tend to fall back on expressions that date from Victorian days, when wordiness was considered a virtue:

at the present	instead of	now
by means of	instead of	by
due to the fact that	instead of	because
during the time that	instead of	while
in the near future	instead of	soon

Probably the wordiness that characterizes undesirable objective writing most often stems from the use of the passive verb, which requires a section of its own.

The Misuse of the Passive

If in your sentence structure up to now, you have employed an animate subject for any action that the person (or thing personified) accomplishes, then you have probably avoided the passive. Passive verbs bury the real subject by dragging the often inanimate object forward and crowning it as the chief noun. We shall devote this section of the chapter to an explanation of this verb form so that you learn to recognize it as you do poison ivy—to avoid it.

There are several legitimate uses of the passive—when you are pursuing one subject in the name of clarity, when you wish to hide the subject, and when you are describing a subject that is actually passive while others act on it. In this situation, for example, a bull *has been tormented* by picadors and the toreador until it stands passive, exhausted and confused. Most often, however, you will find an active verb the better choice.

In the simplest version of our thoughts, a human acts on the inanimate; a human throws the ball. In no way can the ball throw itself. Then how does a sports announcer arrive at this sentence?

> The ball was snapped to first base, putting Casey out.

Here we see the earmarks of the passive verb: an auxiliary of *to be (was),* the verb in the past tense, and the implication of a causative—*by X.* (The object of *by* indicates the basic subject. The phrase may be omitted, although it is always implied and may be replaced.)

Then who threw the ball? Bill, we'll say, a rank-and-file outfielder on the visiting team.

As the image flashed through the announcer's mind, it rose in two differentiated thoughts, roughly like this:

1. <u>Bill</u> snapped the ball to (the) first base(man). That throw put Casey out.

Casey, the home team's star hitter, is a friend of the announcer and a favorite with the local listeners. Without conscious thought, the announcer's mind accomplishes these changes:

2. The ball was snapped <u>by Bill</u> to (the) first base(man). (The) first base(man) put Casey out.

Poor Bill has been switched from subject of the sentence to object of the preposition <u>by</u>. The first baseman, doing no more than his duty, hardly registers.

3. The ball was snapped to first base. That throw put Casey out.

The announcer's mind has linked the two thoughts, in the process dropping both Bill and the first baseman. As he focuses on the important fact, the announcer robs Bill of all credit, and the ball becomes the grammatical subject of the first sentence.

4. The ball was snapped to first base, putting Casey out.

Scientists believe that in the process of forming sentences we follow such processes as these, called *transformations*.

To reverse the transformation, to restore the basic subject of a sentence, you have only to switch ends if the *by* phrase has not been omitted. If it has, then you must replace it before reversing the transformation:

> Jim was kissed under the mistletoe.
> Jim was kissed by Sue under the mistletoe.
> Sue kissed Jim under the mistletoe.

It might matter to someone just who kissed whom!

Remember that the *by* preposition must be *causative;* its object must have produced the effect:

> The house was built by a famous architect.
> The house was built by a waterfall.

An important reason to avoid the passive lies in its tendency to supply too many subjects in a paragraph. To show you what we mean, we'll over-simplify. Group A shows active voice; group B, passive.

A.   1) The boy pondered the possibilities of raising the money.
2) He could ask his father for an advance.
3) He could talk his mother into a loan.
4) He might be able to earn it.
5) Perhaps he could sell his shotgun.
6) He could even sell his stereo.
7) He might talk the hospital into buying his blood.

B.   The <u>boy</u> pondered the possibilities of raising the money. His <u>father</u> could be asked for an advance. His <u>mother</u> might be talked into a loan. <u>To earn</u> it might be possible. His <u>shotgun</u> could perhaps be sold. His <u>stereo</u> could even be sold. The <u>hospital</u> might be talked into buying his blood.

In seven sentences, the passive verb results in seven different subjects. While they are clear enough in this simple example, under ordinary circumstances they may easily confuse a reader.

For the novice writer, the use of the passive voice is something like arsenic-eating. Mid-European women in the last century occasionally nibbled arsenic to give their hair gloss and sheen. Some coachmen fed it to horses. Too much, however, and like them, you might find the passive similarly lethal to the life of your writing.

The Solutions: Vigorous Verbs and Memorable Nouns

Those of our readers who believe that objectivity is essential may protest:

"But I have to write about abstractions! How can I use active verbs with inanimate subjects?"

The answer is simply to presume that your sentences' subjects *can* take an action they suggest, as in the following somewhat exaggerated examples written by a group of computer technicians.

1. The print wire snaps toward a ribbon when the magnetic field is cancelled.
2. Up to four channel adapters reside in the 7306-MM.
3. The printer spewed forth papers.
4. Check-circuits snare the error conditions.
5. Excessive current will explode the land pattern on the circuit board.
6. An error halts processing, then freezes the registers to allow the processor to make a complete log.
7. The interrupt handler jumps to action in response to the interrupt request.
8. The mag card slides into the block.

Note the active verbs in the following paragraph:

> Each transmission reaches the communications controller (the NCP) with a prefix identifying the destination as a binary number. The NCP receives this data, identifies the destination by the binary number, and schedules the data to be transmitted to the appropriate terminal. The NCP handles everything: translation, device codes, line scheduling, error retries, and recovery.[2]

Verbs can be vigorous—but how can nouns be improved? Let's see one method.

Considerable changes have occurred in technical teminology since the computer and the general public found each other. So long as writers discussed cybernetics with readers possessed of equal expertise, they employed the nomenclature common to the industry. When the magic-making chips introduced the micro-computer, they generated a readership of novice and amateur programmers unable to comprehend computer terminology. Consequently, experts began to introduce dozens of terms that suggested amusing analogies—easy to remember. Dictionaries were compiled to explain these phrases that so effectively remained in the reader's mind.

Because there's an object-lesson here for those of us who do ordinary writing, we list some of them, regretting that we cannot give space to their so neatly-appropriate meanings.

daisy chain	load-and-go
Darlington	Drop-dead halt
crippled leapfrog	flip-flop
boot	Cheshire Cat store
deadly embrace	chopper
hex pad	slow death
mail box	pingpong

If a test you must make of a program were called crippled leapfrog, wouldn't that bring a smile even to the onerous job of testing?

Incidentally, this brand-new field of computer writing bears out what you might term our "hang-up" with three's. The reader finds triads everywhere: third-generation computer (of three generations), three-addresses, three-D process, three-plus-one address, three-input adder.

In some respects, the scientific brains that produce such marvels as the micro-chip are little different from those that wrote all those nursery rhymes.

Our advice is intended to apply also to those writers in the next group, whose option for objectivity often results in what an authority disdains as "boredom, a deadly dullness, ambiguity, lifelessness, and poor readability—all the characteristics of the 'old school' of writing."

WRITING DIRECTIVES

In one of his short stories, Kipling refers to a man and his wife and a Tertium Quid—that is, a whole made up of two halves and something extra. Subjective and objective writing can be thought of as such a whole; this third group is the something extra that all too often employs the formal objective in a subjective situation.

It is from this last group that so often come the least defensible examples of frustrated communication, made public by knowledgeable individuals who deplore such writing. In its column "Gobbledygook," the Washington, D.C., *Star* featured an excerpt from bureaucratic directives like the following every day for several years.

> A question has arisen about the amount of recent increase in employee remuneration (a matter, regrettably, of only 2%) that has asked and received the most careful consideration. After much thought, it becomes obvious that such an increase must be appreciated as much in the abstract as in the concrete; that is, it is an acknowledged recognition of the merits of those who receive it. The effective date has been delayed four months into the fiscal year for reasons that cannot now be publicized, although they assuredly stem from good salary administration and due concern for the merit system.

Since such a writer often possesses certain information about his readers—job description, salary range, probable education—you'd expect him to take the subjective approach. All too often, he elects to distance himself in the formality of passive verbs and abstract nouns. He may do so for several reasons.

1. Perhaps he generalizes that, to address many people, it seems necessary to move higher into abstractions, just as in arithmetic, we must move higher to find the lowest common denominator between 3 and 328. (Similarly, to write a thesis that covers and links three main points, we raise our "umbrella"; i.e., we generalize.)

2. Perhaps he simply wants this directive to sound authoritative and to reflect his superior standing.

3. Perhaps he is convinced that the gravity of the subject is best suited by an objective approach.

The plant manager who dictated the following memo probably was simply angry; he'd have to account to the board for the added expense of the guards.

> Starting March 1, all personnel should be advised that the services of Guaranteed Protection Company have been engaged to provide two guards nightly to patrol the building and grounds. Unauthorized personnel will not be admitted after working hours without a special pass which they must produce from their supervisors, or unless their names are on a supervisors' list that will be checked by the guards. The costly pilferage of supplies and the misuse of equipment for pesonal benefit at night has got to stop.

Had he considered his words more carefully, he might have worded his directive more like this:

> As I'm sure you'll agree, the company must check the continuing nightly pilferage of supplies and the misuse of equipment for personal benefit. We all know that replacement and repair can slow down production, a cause of concern to everyone.
>
> Beginning March 1, then, if you find you must return to the building after hours, please see your supervisor for a pass that our two new night-watchmen will collect.
>
> P.S. John, the watchmen will have your name on a special list. Just show your I.D.

The subjective tone and the postscript for those on the "preferred" list suggest a more effective approach than the objective distancing.

Not always are the ills of over-objectivity limited to short memos, however. Most often they occur in large-scale directives like instruction manuals, which are written by professionals who understand their jargon very well. Unfortunately, such writers fail to make allowances for inexperienced readers, as in the following examples.

Laura's Handbook

Bee is a supervisor for the New Dakota state welfare department, unmarried and in her mid-30s, pleasant in manner and appearance. She is dedicated to her job and anxious to give it her best efforts.

Her degree in sociology was earned at a woman's college, where she proved exceptionally conscientious. That same characteristic has aided her advance to her present position.

One of Bee's responsibilities is to pass on the many changes in welfare directives as they descend from both federal and state legislation. Faithfully, she writes up these changes as they apply to her particular area; then, after they are printed, she whisks out copies to workers in the field. They in turn carefully insert the new sheaf of directives in their Handbook.

The Handbook, a looseleaf binder some two inches thick, directs each social worker as she copes with her clients' many problems. In the Handbook are defined all the possibilities she might encounter, along with the controlling regulations. Although new pages are always being added, far fewer are ever deemed safe to remove.

Such a Handbook is a permanent occupant of the shotgun seat in Laura Byrd's car. Diana-like Laura, 22 and bright-eyed with excitement about her first job, plans to be the most dedicated "eligibility specialist" in the state's child welfare program. The day she received the Handbook, she resolved to memorize every word of it. After a weekend's study, she felt less confident. Now, whenever she has to look up something, she feels strongly reluctant to search through material like this:

> At the time eligibility is determined and at each redetermination of eligibility, the caretaker of the eligible child(ren) must be informed that any child support payments received from an absent parent which are covered by the assignment of support rights must be paid directly to the Clerk of Superior Court (CSC) within five days after receipt. Also inform the caretaker of the sanctions for refusing to cooperate.

> A recipient has a right to a notice ten (10) calendar days in advance of a proposal to terminate or reduce his assistance and he has a right to have an opportunity to discuss the proposed action in a conference with a member of the county department of social services, except for situations indicated in IIA below and suspected fraud situations (in which case a five-calendar day advance notice is mailed to the recipient).

> The caretaker-relative must understand that the assignment of rights to support applies to all applicants and recipients of AFDC regardless of whether the reason for deprivation of the child(ren) for whom assistance is claimed is due to death, incapacity, or absence from the home. Referral to the local IV-D agency is made only when an absent parent has deserted or abandoned the child(ren).

More than once, in some desperate situation involving a frantic mother and sad-eyed children, Laura has planned to lodge a protest against the Handbook. Why can't it address her specifically? Why such convoluted sentences? Why are the subjects of its sentences so often the recipient of the action?

If she survives until she gains some seniority, she vows, she'll insist on instructions that sound friendly and helpful. More important, they'll make clear what workers are supposed to do. (She doesn't as yet know the complications involved.)

Consider that first excerpt from the Handbook. Although the first sentence has a staggering 55 words, it is entirely grammatical. What is its subject? The caretaker. And the verb? *must be informed*. Then who does the informing? Who is the real subject? We reverse the passive transformation:

> The caretaker must be informed (by the eligibility specialist).
> The eligibility specialist must inform the caretaker. ...

In other words, *Laura* is the real subject; she must take action.

The two sentences in that one paragraph total 66 words. Do you find this 48-word paragraph more acceptable?

> Whenever the child's eligibility is determined or redetermined, you should inform his caretaker of two facts: (1) If she has received any assigned child support payments from an absent parent, she must pay them directly to the Clerk of Superior Court. (2) She will be penalized if she does not.

Almost always, the use of a passive verb involves unnecessary wordiness.

If we pointed out to Bee that Laura is not as familiar with jargon as she is, and that any instructions intended for an individual should properly be addressed to that individual, what would she say?

She would flush, perhaps, and protest that her sentences are grammatically correct. If she were pressed, she might explain:

> "Oh, but that's the way the regulations read! That's the way the lawyers worded these restrictions ... Just suppose I might misinterpret something!"

Bee's concern centers on her personal record, rather than on Laura's comprehension. She should set a picture of Laura on her desk to remind her for whom she writes.

What can we learn from Bee's situation?
1. To clarify is more important than to impress (and mystify).
2. To depend on passive verbs is to throw away the subject and lose the action of the verb.
3. To write jargon sentences of more than twenty words will lose or confuse most readers.

THE WHO-FOR
TEMPLATE REVERSED

Such over-use of objectivity is no more Bee's shortsightedness than that of her superiors and teachers. In turn, they have followed the writing patterns set in the early stages of what are now called the social services, when their professors (in both senses) and readers were often very learned men. It is time to realize that such writing today must reach many readers whose education has been geared less intensively and in other directions.

Instead of the old patterns, everyone would benefit if writers of this third group were to analyze the situation in terms of our most recent template *(Who for? What for? Why for?).* Unlike the former situation involving Ian Keith, for writers like Bee, the questions should be directed to the *problem.*

What is the problem?
Why is it a problem?
Who solves this problem?

In Bee's situation, we would generate the following answers:

What is the problem?	To get these latest changes in policy regulated.
Why is it a problem?	The new regulations are written in legalese, with the recipients of the benefits as the persons most concerned. Bee's job is to inform the worker how to tell who is eligible for those benefits, to translate the legalese. She is writing instructions about making decisions of considerable importance.
Who will solve the problem?	Eligibility workers (her readers), who may have limited experience and training (possibly with no college background). They need clear, unambiguous information, direct guidelines.

With such an analysis, Bee might rewrite the following sentence (excerpted from the Handbook) as it appears in the second version, half as long—but still lengthy.

1. The federal IV-D regulations state that when a family for whom child support payments have been collected and distributed under Title IV-D ceases to receive AFDC, the IV-D agency (IV-D Accounting) may continue to collect support payments from the absent parent and distribute the money to the family *if the client has authorized the IV-D agency to do so.* (61 words)

2. IV-D may continue collecting support payments from an absent parent for a remaining parent and children even if they cease to receive AFDC, federal regulations say, provided the caretaker so authorizes. (31 words)

Wordiness might have been a virtue in Victorian novels, but the attention span of contemporary readers seems to lessen every year. We remember when a given TV picture could remain on the screen for 18 seconds; now the count is more likely to be 5 or 6.

In vetoing wordiness, we find an analogy also in directions advised for the computer programmer. Under the subhead "Every word counts in computer language," eminent authority Walter H. Buchsbaum writes:

> A word in the English language may often contribute very little to the sentence in which it appears. It may be vague, redundant, or totally erroneous. However, the sentence itself will still be understandable and will get itself across. In a computer language, all words are unambiguous and, if they appear in the program code, will have a predictable impact on the proceedings.

Buchsbaum goes on to say that "word," although not generally found in computer languages, is a "buzz word" in the industry, equivalent to a set of characters that are represented in 16 bits (two bytes). The only way to keep some Group 3 writers from excessive wordiness, it seems, is to fine them 16 bits for each unnecessary word—a matter of $2.00!

Deric's Need to Keep Awake

In terms of addressing a problem to unknown readers, few writing assignments require more varied skills than technological instruction manuals. The writers of such books must be more than usually competent in knowledge of their subject, yet skillful also in expressing the increments of learning. To be logical is not enough; they must somehow manage to maintain the reader's interest. Like all proceed-at-your-own-pace texts, the great problem is boredom, multiplied exponentially in the case of computer jargon. The expedients that differentiate it from the common grayness, then, should serve to activate all kinds of inert jargon.

Let's picture Deric, a new technician trainee who will eventually service the industrial computers leased by his employers, a great computer manufacturer. He will, that is, if he isn't fired for falling asleep over the keyboard. He calls his nightly practice hours The Everglades, for the study material offers little light and even less sure footing.

By company standards the instructions in his training manuals are expressed acceptably if impersonally like this:

> ACF provides for multiple-system (or multiple-domain) networks. Such a network consists of multiple single-domain networks tied together via channel connections or SDLC links. In the multiple-domain network, several access methods (ACF/VTAMs or ACF/TCAMs) share ownership of the network resources. In addition, "cross-domain" sessions are supported. That is, a resource owned by one access method can be in session with a resource owned by another access method.[3]

Even with the short sentences and active verbs, Deric finds himself nodding at times when the abstract expressions seem to run together.

Is there a means of enlivening such bone-dry instruction? Yes, his employers have decided; writers could make better use of analogy, and they could write as if they were addressing Deric face to face. Now Deric's successors will read elementary training manuals that are less soporific:

A.   In this Edgar Users Guide, you'll find out how to summon editorial skills needed for a finished, print-ready document.

       Just as you interpret and obey traffic signals, so EDGAR will react to your previously programmed commands. Like you, EDGAR responds to varying signals as it "drives" through your data, performing tasks you've earmarked.

B. You should think of the Primary/Secondary concept as similar to a telephone conference call, when several stations on the line communicate with one particular station.

In this link-up, the network control program is the Primary Station. As the host, it's like the Chairman of the Board. All other stations on the link are secondary stations, subordinates who do not speak without an invitation.[4]

Writers of material intended for readers of less expertise in their profession's jargon must remember their real goal: communication. The best technical instructions come to naught if they fail to engage the reader's interest and comprehension.

THE FINAL PARALLEL
OF THE COMPUTER ANALOGY

As we have maintained throughout this book, you serve your interests best when you take care to communicate with your reader, to "program" him to your way of thinking. Our analogy of the professional computer programmer is basically sound, for he is compelled to consider the computer's need to understand. If he doesn't address its requirements, his writing effort fails. While our loss may not be immediate, it may have the same result.

In fact, our own carelessness in writing is best paralleled when the computer fails to communicate with *us*. We grind our teeth when it won't understand—when it won't heed our protests that it's making some mistake—usually financial. (Perhaps the programmer didn't write with sufficient care!) Without thought for our own weaknesses in written communication, we laugh at the dozens of stories of computer "misbehavior," much like those that parents tell about their children.

(There's the one about the stubborn computer, for example, that kept billing a department-store customer for $0.00—until the customer mailed it a check for that amount!)

Now, when a computer badgers you, you can turn to your home computer for rescue. A book entitled *Computer Programs in BASIC* (Prentice-Hall, 1981) by Paul Friedman enables you to generate a form letter that you mail in return!

The computer scores again.

SUMMARY

Most managerial writing needs to be reader-oriented, rather than coldly formal. Even though the material is to be read by unknown subordinates or strangers (as in directives or instructions), it should avoid the worst aspects of objectivity:

leaden passive verbs, wordiness, obscure diction. The writer should not stray into jargon unless the reader is certain to understand it.

If formal objectivity is essential, the writer can employ third-person subjects (as in this sentence), linking them to carefully chosen verbs that provide the illusion of action. Even technical writing achieves warmth and readability by vigorous verbs and effective comparisons.

ASSIGNMENTS

1. Write a list of the characteristics expected of employees in your office. Make the various items parallel, and add bullets for emphasis.

2. In your newspaper, check the Letters to the Editor column, sorting out those that need improvement. Apply the principles brought out in this and the foregoing chapter and rewrite several.

3. Choose an editorial with which you disagree and, answering the specific issues it raises, write an editorial in reply.

4. The following paragraph from a social services office should be shortened and clarified. Begin by jotting down a rough digest in list form of each sentence. Has the paragraph a topic sentence? Does the material follow in logical order? Do you agree that the underlined material is most important? Rewrite the paragraph after applying the formula to it. Avoid repetition and keep your sentence length as close to twenty words as you can.

You may wish to use these synonyms for the legal terms:

arrearage: amount owed in payment, a debt, a deficiency
indemnification: compensation, repayment
subsequent: following in time or order, coming after, since

(1) The IV-D Program [AFDC] agency is entitled to seek indeminfication for public assistance granted subsequent to 6/30/75 under the authority of GS 110-135. (2) The amount of past public assistance should be determined at the time a support obligation is established, and this amount should be included in the initial court order obtained by the IV-D agency. (3) The past paid assistance amount then becomes a legally established arrearage. (4) Past public assistance does not constitute an arrearage which may be enforced and collected until it is included in a court order. (5) *If there is a prior support order which existed during the time that past public assistance was paid, the debt to the State is limited to the amount of this order, and the amount of past public assistance which may be established as arrearage cannot exceed the total amount owed under this order.* (6) If the amount of past public assistance for a child is $726 ($121 for six months), but during this time the absent parent was under an order to pay $50 per month to the mother, the total amount of past public assistance that can be recovered is $300. (7) If the amount of past public assistance is less than the court-ordered arrearage, any amount of the arrearage over and above the amount of past public assistance is non-AFDC-arrears and owed to the mother by the father.

NOTES

1. Herman M. Weisman, *Technical Correspondence* (New York: John Wiley & Sons, 1968), pp. 22-23.
2. Used by permission of IBM.
3. Used by permission of IBM.
4. Used by permission of IBM.

SELECTED
BIBLIOGRAPHY

As you become more skilled at writing, you will find the following works particularly helpful:

Biagi, Shirley, *How to Write and Sell Magazine Articles*. Englewood Cliffs, N,.J.: Prentice-Hall, Inc., 1981.

Blicq, Ronald. *Guidelines for Report Writers: A Complete Manual for On-the-Job Report Writing*. Englewood Cliffs, N.J.: Prentice-Hall, Inc., 1982.

Kelsch, Mary L. and Thomas Kelsch. *Writing Effectively: A Practical Guide*. Englewood Cliffs, N.J.: Prentice-Hall, Inc., 1981.

Lanham, Richard A. *Revising Prose*. New York: Charles Scribner & Sons, 1979.

Strunk, William, and White, E. B. *The Elements of Style,* 3rd ed. New York: Macmillan, 1978.

Trimble, John R. *Writing with Style: Conversations on the Art of Writing*. Englewood Cliffs, N.J.: Prentice-Hall, Inc., 1975.

Weathers, Winston, and Otis Winchester. *The Strategy of Style*. New York: McGraw-Hill, 1967.

Zinsser, William. *On Writing Well: An Informal Guide to Writing Nonfiction*. New York: Harper & Row, 1980.

Because an understanding of computer programming seems essential today even for those readers who never plan to write a program, we also recommend:

Conway, Richard, and others. *Programming for Poets: A Gentle Introduction to Pascal*. Cambridge, Mass: Winthrop Publishers, Inc., 1980.

INDEX

NOW ... Announcing these other fine books from Prentice-Hall—

A WRITER'S GUIDE: Easy Ground Rules for Successful Written English, by Jane Walpole. From writing a simple independent clause to handling a split infinitive, this book explains all the concepts of grammar in a clear, logical way. Covers punctuation, syntax, the seven parts of speech, clauses and phrases, verb forms and tenses, sentence structure, and spelling.

$4.95 paperback, $9.95 hardcover

TECHNICAL WRITING FOR BEGINNERS by Winston Smock. A style handbook for the beginning technical writer, this book features a step-by-step description of the technical publishing process from the inception of a writing project to the delivery of printed copies. Covers research, writing, revision, editing, production, and printing.

$5.95 paperback, $12.95 hardcover

To order these books, just complete the convenient order form below and mail to **Prentice-Hall, Inc., General Publishing Division, Attn. Addison Tredd, Englewood Cliffs, N.J. 07632**

Title	Author	Price*

Subtotal _____

Sales Tax (where applicable) _____

Postage & Handling (75¢/book) _____

Total $ _____

Please send me the books listed above. Enclosed is my check ☐ Money order ☐ or, charge my VISA ☐ MasterCard ☐ Account #_____

Credit card expiration date _____

Name _____

Address _____

City _____ State _____ Zip _____

Prices subject to change without notice. Please allow 4 weeks for delivery.